Interesting Stories for Curious Minds 2

A Book of Fascinating Trivia, Short Stories & Fun Facts for Adults, Volume 2

Margaret Lashley

Published by Zazzy Ideas, Inc., 2023.

Copyright

Introduction

Hello again!

Welcome back to the second edition of *Interesting Stories for Curious Minds*—your gateway to random, absurd, and oddly hilarious facts about the people and places we share our planet with!

While researching for my mystery novels, I've uncovered yet another treasure trove of stories you probably won't find anywhere else.

Come along and share in the fun! The world is truly a fascinating place. So kick back, get comfy, and get ready to laugh while you learn.

All my best,

Margaret Lashley

P.S. If you'd like to learn more about me and my other books, check me out on Amazon or my website, margaretlashley.com. A list of my works is also available on the last page of this book.

Quirky as the Dickens

As a writer myself, I'll admit we "artist types" can be a tad eccentric. For example, I once worked at a major newspaper where my editor couldn't do anything until he'd sharpened twenty No. 2 pencils to pinpoints and lined them up on his desk like a miniature, orange life raft. (A Freudian wish to escape, perhaps?)

Anyway, let's just say that an artist's solitary profession can encourage ... *odd habits*. How odd? You be the judge as we take a look at some famous artists with rather infamous quirks:

Theodor Seuss Geisel. Better known as Dr. Seuss, he's the prolific author and illustrator of classic children's books such as *The Cat in the Hat*. Apparently, Seuss was quite fond of head coverings himself. At his abode he kept a "secret closet" stocked with nearly 300 hats. Whenever he felt writer's block coming on, he'd go inside his closet and choose a hat to wear until he felt inspired again. Hats off (or maybe, hats on) to Dr. Seuss!

Charles Dickens. The author of *A Tale of Two Cities* and *A Christmas Carol* may have been haunted by his own ghosts from the past. Dickens' writing schedule was rigid and peculiar. From precisely 9 a.m. to 2 p.m., he religiously put pen to paper—and the house had to remain completely silent the entire time.

But that was just step one in his writing process. Like my boss at the paper, Dickens' pens and ink had to be arranged just so on his desk. So did a small collection of statuettes. The little figures had to be lined up perfectly on Dickens desk because they "helped him think."

Dickens took the statuettes wherever he traveled. When he stayed in hotels and guesthouses, he moved the furniture around to recreate the layout of his home office as closely as possible. In addition, he would only sleep facing north. Why? Dickens believed facing north better aligned him to the electrical currents of the Earth. Sort of shocking, eh?

Maya Angelou. Famed poet and author of *I Know Why the Caged Bird Sings* might have felt a little cagey herself. She couldn't write at home. Finding the comfort of her house too distracting, she sought out what she described as "tiny, mean" hotel rooms. The humble, bare quarters helped sharpen her focus.

She'd rent them for months at a time, but she didn't spend the night in them. Instead, Angelou would arrive early each morning armed with a Bible, her writing materials, a bottle of sherry, and a deck of cards. She claimed the cards helped busy her "little mind" while she pondered and wrote, often while reclining on her side on the hotel bed. She once confessed to the *Paris Review* that one of her elbows was rough with callouses from lying on it for endless hours every day. Huh. Maybe she should've used more elbow grease...

Salvador Dali. A definitive master of the surrealism art movement of the 1910s and 1920s, Dali sought to tap into his unconscious mind to access treasures buried deep within his imagination. The melting clocks in his masterwork, *The Persistence of Memory,* bear witness to his attempt to capture the blurry line between dreams and reality.

How did Dali reach his odd perspectives on the world around him? One way was by chasing dreams. He would hold a key over a metal pan as he napped. When he nodded off and dropped the key, the clatter would wake him up. In this twilight state, he'd quickly jot down the strange images flashing through his mind.

Another method Dali employed was to intentionally brood over bizarre and illogical thoughts in order to reach a state of "concrete irrationality." Dali would then paint the strange visions still lingering in his mind's eye. (Well, that explains a lot, doesn't it?)

Ludwig Van Beethoven. Though dead for over 200 years, the works of this masterful German composer still rank among the top classical music pieces performed today. What was his secret? It could've been something as simple as coffee.

Beethoven began each day with a breakfast of only coffee, obsessively counting out 60 beans by hand to make the brew. Afterward, he would work for a few hours at his desk before heading out on long, meandering walks through the countryside.

As inspiration struck, he'd jot down notes in a large sketchbook. Beethoven may also have composed works while bathing. His secretary, Anton Schindler, reported that Beethoven would pace around his room, pouring jugs of water over his hands as he hummed tunes and stared into space in deep meditation. I wonder, could he have been in a singsong trance?

Fun Fact: In 1956, Chuck Berry wrote a hit song called *Roll Over Beethoven*. In it, Berry tells the DJ to stop playing classical music and put on hit rock and roll songs instead. It must've worked. Since then, Berry's catchy song has been performed by The Beatles (1963), Electric Light Orchestra (1973), and Keith Richards (2015), to name a few.

On another note, Beethoven may indeed, be rolling over in his grave right now. Especially if he finds out that a modified version of his Piano Sonata No. 27 is being used as the intro music to the *Judge Judy* TV show.

Would You Take a Buck for That?

Who doesn't like a bargain? Flea markets, yard sales, thrift shops and garage sales are some of the best places to find them. But if you thought you lucked out getting that 10-speed bike for $25, the deals some folks have stumbled upon could leave your heart racing with envy.

Below are some of the most mind-blowing treasures ever found at bargain venues. The return on investment generated by some of them is enough to make even a Rockefeller turn over in his grave.

A Head for Money. In 1989, a painting of two flowers was purchased for $29 at a garage sale by a Wisconsin man. It was later identified as a work by Martin Johnson Heade (1819-1904) entitled, *Two Magnolias on Blue Plush.* In 1999, the lucky guy who found it sold it at a Christie's auction for $882,500.

Priceless Declaration. In 1989, a man paid $4 for a torn painting at a flea market. Buying it for its frame, he discarded the picture and found a folded-up paper inside. It turned out to be one of 200 original copies of the *Declaration of Independence* ordered by Congress back in 1820. In 1991, he sold it for $2.42 million.

A Peach of a Pair. At a garage sale in Philadelphia, a man handed over $35 for two small paintings. As it turned out, the artist was John F. Kensett (1816-1872). Together, the paintings were valued at $100,000.

Declaration Duo. You would think finding a copy of the original *Declaration of Independence* would be a one-off, right? But in 2007, a man shopping at a thrift shop in Tennessee bought an old document and a pair of salt and pepper shakers for the tidy sum of $2.48. Upon further investigation, he realized he, too, had found one of the 200 originals. He sold it at auction for an undisclosed sum.

Black & White Gold. In 2000, at a garage sale in Fresno California, Rick Norsigian paid $45 for two boxes containing 65 old photo negatives. The images are believed to have been taken by celebrated artist Ansel Adams (1902-1984). The collection has been valued at $200 million.

One-of-a-Kind Punk. In 2002, Warren Hill bought a Velvet Underground album in a sidewalk sale. Shelling out 75 cents for it, he figured he'd gotten a bargain, as the CD was selling for $7 on Amazon. But upon closer inspection, he realized the record was a demo that Lou Reed's trailblazing punk group had cut for Columbia Records back in April 1966. The only known copy of the recording session, Hill sold it on eBay for $25,000.

Treasure for a Song. In 2007, a family in New York paid $3 for a five-and-a-half inch white bowl. It sat on their mantle gathering dust until they discovered it was a priceless piece of porcelain from China's Northern Song Dynasty. In 2013, they sold it at a Sotheby's auction for $2.2 million.

Dandy Andy. In 2010, while visiting Las Vegas, British businessman Andy Fields bought a child's drawing from a yard sale for $5. The picture was of 1930s singer Rudy Vallee. And the artist? A young Andy Warhol. The famous artist had sketched it at age 10 or 11, when he was sick in bed with cholera. Fields hasn't sold the sketch yet, but the work of art is estimated to be worth $2 million.

Playing Hardball. A man antiquing in Baileyville, Maine struck a bargain on a photo album, some old Coca-Cola bottles, and a couple of oak chairs, paying less than $100 for the lot. Inside the album he found an original 1865 photograph showing nine Brooklynite baseball players and a manager—considered by the Library of Congress to be the very first dated baseball card. One of only two known to exist, the rare memorabilia sold at auction for $92,000.

Passport to Riches. In 2013, a man at an estate sale in Detroit, Michigan paid 50 cents for a vinyl record. Upon further inspection, he found the 1964 passport of Marvin Gaye tucked inside the cover. It's been valued at $20,000.

You Buddha Believe It! In 1997, like a lot of people rummaging through a garage sale in St. Louis, a woman almost passed up the battered bronze statue. But something made her cough up the $100 asking price. Little did she know the Buddha statue was made in the 15th century, and was thought to be of imperial quality. When she found out, she put the statue up for auction, expecting to make $80,000. The final hammer came down at a cool $2.1 million.

Fun Fact: The highest know price paid for a painting at auction was $450.3 million. It was for Leonardo da Vinci's *Salvator Mundi*, painted circa 1500.

Wanna be a Slang Slinger?

It's tough to stay cool. (Actually, just using that phrase may mark me as un-cool.) If you'd like to stay on trend with the latest pop-culture terminology, or you'd merely like to embarrass the stew out of the young hipsters in your life, here's a guide to the latest catchwords you should be spouting.

These nine words should keep you on trend—at least until the end of 2023:

1. *Boujee*. (To be rich, special, fancy.) "He's so boujee driving that Tesla."

2. *Bussin'*. (Really good, amazing.) "This gluten-free, vegan burrito is totally bussin.'"

3. *Dripping*. (Stylish, sophisticated clothing or look.) "Emma's purse and belt are dripping."

4. *Extra*. (Dramatic, attention-grabbing. Or too much.) "Bro, you don't have to be so extra about it!"

5. *Rent-Free*. (To dominate one's thoughts, become an obsession.) "Ever since I heard that Billie Eilish tune on the radio, he's been living rent-free inside my head."

6. *Salty*. (To overreact.) "When I didn't text him back right away, he got all salty."

7. *Shook*. (Shocked, stunned.) "That final episode of *The Watcher* has me shook."

8. *Vibe Check*. (To make sure someone's having a good time.) Dude: "Hey, Bro, vibe check!" Bro: "All good, Dude."

9. *Woke*. (Socially conscious, culturally aware.) "After hearing about what the other person had been through, he became woke to another point of view."

Fun Fact: Here are some other common slang words you can still look fly saying this year. (FYI, "looking fly" isn't one of them.)

- Amped (excited)
- Basic (boring)
- Chill or Chill Out (relax)
- Cray or Cray-Cray. (crazy, wild)
- Epic (incredible, awesome)
- Hang Out (spend time with)
- I Can't Even (overwhelmed with)
- Legit (good or worthwhile)
- YOLO (you only live once)
- Zone Out (get distracted)

Lowly Litter-Bug Earns Tidy Sum

Coming up with a brilliant idea usually requires the uncanny ability to "think outside the box." But for Edward Lowe, thinking *inside* the box is what eventually led him to hit pay-dirt.

Born in 1920, Lowe was destined to spend his life working at his family's business in Michigan. As the company sales rep, it was his job to sell sand, sawdust, and clay to heavy-industry clients. (The materials were used to soak up manufacturing-related spills.) Not exactly a glamorous gig, but it paid the bills.

All that changed in the middle of the winter of 1947. One day in January, one of Lowe's neighbors, Mrs. Draper, came over and asked him for some sand for her cat's indoor toilet tray. Lowe explained to her that his sand pile was frozen. He thought that would be the end of the matter. But just like Don Draper on the TV series *Mad Men*, Mrs. Draper wouldn't take "no" for an answer.

Seeking to get rid of her, Lowe's recalled he'd just received a free sample of a new kind of clay. He wasn't interested in it for his business, but he knew about clay's natural absorbency. So Lowe gave Mrs. Draper some of it to appease her. She took it and left.

Problem solved. Or so Lowe thought ...

A few days later, his neighbor was back. This time, instead of complaining, Mrs. Draper told him how great the clay was. She wanted more. Lowe obliged. After she left, he took a closer look at the clay itself. Called Fuller's Earth, it contained a special combination of clay minerals capable of absorbing their weight in water, along with odors.

Soon, Mrs. Draper returned yet again for more clay, this time bringing some friends along with her. They all wanted the clay to replace the sand and ash normally used in their cats' indoor trays.

That's when Lowe had his eureka moment—he would create a new product for *inside* the litter box!

Now, all he had to do was convince cat owners across the nation that clay was better than sand and ash. Given that the two were cheap or even free to obtain, getting customers to pay for clay was going to be a hard sell. (One that might've daunted even Don Draper and his amazing salesmanship.)

Still, Lowe couldn't simply dump the idea. Undaunted, in 1947 he packaged the clay in five-pound bags and called it "Kitty Litter." He took it to a local pet store owner and suggested he sell it for 65 cents (the equivalent of about eight bucks today).

The store owner scoffed at the idea, calling Lowe's product "dirt in a bag." He told Lowe no one would buy it, because sand was so much cheaper.

That could've been it for Lowe's idea. But fortunately, this time, it was *Lowe* who wouldn't take "no" for an answer. Thinking outside the box, he told the pet store owner to give the Kitty Litter away for free—until people were willing to pay for it.

In the meantime, Lowe hit the road with bags of Kitty Litter, driving to cat shows across the country. He was surprised to find the shows stunk to high heaven—due to the animals' urine and feces.

Knowing he had the solution, Lowe cleaned cat boxes at shows to earn booth space to demonstrate his Kitty Litter. People who stopped by were amazed at how his simple clay product helped with the odor. It also didn't track dust like ash or sand.

As Kitty Litter's popularity grew, Lowe founded Edward Lowe Industries. He created *Tidy Cat* box filler in 1964.

Eventually, through Lowe's persistence, cat litter became *the* product that no modern cat owner could live without. By the time of his death in 1995, Lowe's company was worth $500 million (close to a billion in today's dollars). Not bad for a crappy job, eh?

Fun Facts: Still haven't had your fill of kitty litter? Here are some more interesting nuggets to claw through:

◇ Indoor litter boxes didn't come into fashion until the 1940s. Before then, cats did their business outside with the pooches.

◇ As of 2022, over 60.6 million US adults owned a cat. That's 29% of the population!

◇ The 2022 worldwide market for cat litter was estimated at $11.23 billion.

◇ In later years, Lowe worked on developing a chimpanzee litter with Jane Goodall, but was unable to develop a successful product.

◇ Clay litter is now the most used litter in the US.

◇ Every year, we dump around eight billion pounds of cat litter into landfills. Clay cat litter isn't biodegradable, so the poop we dump will probably outlast you and me by centuries.

You Animal You!

Humans like to think of ourselves as evolved species. But other animals show a surprisingly wide range of "human like" behaviors, from compassion to aggression. Check out these antics from our not-so-distant animal cousins:

- Wild dolphins call each other by name.
- Ants have urbanized. New York City has its own species, called the ManhattAnt. It's found nowhere else on Earth!
- Octopuses, considered the most intelligent invertebrate, have been observed using tools.
- At 230 decibels, sperm whales are the loudest animal on Earth. (An airplane is 150 decibels at takeoff.)
- Koala fingerprints are indistinguishable from human fingerprints.
- In the Arctic, polar bears have been mating with grizzlies, making a new animal called the pizzly!
- To prevent themselves from drifting apart, sea otters hold hands while they sleep.
- Butterflies have been known to drink blood.
- Goldfish have great memories.
- Female dragonflies will fake their own death to prevent males from having sex with them.
- Shark babies will devour each other in the womb.

Fun Fact: Humans and animals share even more surprising abilities. Did you know we are capable of echolocation, just like a bat or a whale? Also, our jaws have enough power to bite off our own fingers, bone and all. The only thing stopping us is our brain's innate safety factor.

Rocking Out Completely

Ivittuut, Greenland doesn't look like a place where anything much would ever happen. As it stands today, the place is just a scant handful of abandoned buildings sitting along a remote, frigid coastline 1,244 miles from the North Pole.

Yet a closer look at the buildings of Ivittuut reveal they encircle a gigantic, round hole in the earth—a crater that looks for all the world like ground zero for an asteroid strike. What gives?

While it wasn't an asteroid that made the crater, the hole *did* cause a planet-wide extinction—the very first (and so far only) of its kind in the entire world.

The massive pit in the ground is actually a man-made quarry. And, like the blast left behind by some super-villain's diabolical weapon, this mining operation single-handedly spelled the end of the line for a mineral called cryolite.

Not to be confused with kryptonite (Superman's Achilles heel) cryolite nevertheless possesses its own kind of super powers. For instance:

◇ Cryolite is denser than quartz, yet it's often as transparent or translucent as ice (or as white as chunks of snow).

◇ Cryolite stems from the Greek words kryos (ice) and lithos (stone). So cryolite literally means, "ice stone."

◇ Greenland's indigenous Inuit call cryolite "the ice that never melts." (Makes me wonder if this is what Superman's icy Fortress of Solitude was *really* made of.)

◇ Underwater, cryolite's glassy, refractive qualities act like a cloaking device, making it virtually invisible to spot while submerged.

◈ Cryolite can be used as a natural insecticide and pesticide. (Take *that*, Mothman!)

But these cool qualities weren't what led to cryolite's demise. It was actually something much more pedestrian; the manufacturing of aluminum.

Back in the mid-1800s, metallurgists realized the enormous industrial potential of lightweight aluminum. The problem was, alumina (aluminum oxide) was usually found in bauxite deposits, and it was hard to separate the two.

A breakthrough in 1884 by American and French chemists found molten cryolite made it easy and inexpensive to extract metallic aluminum via the process of electrolysis. Naturally, this caused demand for cryolite to skyrocket.

The mine at Ivittuut was the planet's *only* motherlode.

Over the next 50 years, work at the mine continued in earnest. Because of Greenland's frigid climate, miners flooded the quarry pit each autumn to prevent it from filling with snow. Each spring, they would break the ice on top and pump out the water. From April to October, the cryolite-rich ore would be extracted, then loaded on ships heading to ports in Europe, Canada, and the US.

Over the years, the mine expanded to a 1,500-foot-long inclined tunnel, some portions lying 200 feet below the frigid sea. In 1962, after producing 3.7 million tons of ore graded 58% cryolite, the deposits were declared to be mined out. After cleaning up the site, the mine in Ivittuut was abandoned in 1987.

In 2010, the US Geological Survey reported that there were no cryolite reserves left. In other words, cryolite had been mined to extinction. (Not even Superman could save it.)

The only other places cryolite has ever been found (and then only in small quantities) are in Spain, the foot of Pikes Peak in Colorado, Miask, Russia, and a quarry near Montreal in Quebec, Canada. Today, cryolite has been replaced. Synthetic sodium aluminum fluoride is now produced from the common mineral fluorite.

Fun Fact: In 2022, a team of researchers in Somalia discovered two new minerals that have never been seen on Earth before. These new-to-science minerals were identified from a 2.5 ounce slice removed from a 16.5 ton meteorite—the ninth largest ever found. Welcome to Earth, *elaliite* (named for the town El Ali, where the meteorite was found), and *ekinstantonite* (named after Lindy Elkins-Tanton, professor at Arizona State University's School of Earth and Space Exploration).

Chicken Little was Right

If you've ever experienced a hail storm, tornado, or a hurricane, you have first-hand experience with how cranky Mother Nature can get. Given the right conditions, winds can crank up and hurl objects around as big as busses.

But sometimes, Mother Nature likes to play tricks on us and drop things out of the clear blue sky for no apparent reason. What gives? Here are a list of bizarre objects that fell out of the sky with no warning, whatsoever:

Meat Flakes. Like something out of a bad sequel to *Cloudy with a Chance of Meatballs*, in 1876 the people of Olympian Springs, Kentucky were inundated by odd flakes falling from the sky. Two men (of course they were *men*) tasted the flakes and reported they had the flavor of mutton or venison. It couldn't have been some poor ground-up goose caught in an airplane engine—planes hadn't been invented yet. The only explanation they could come up with was that it was vulture vomit!

Golf Balls. In 1969, in Punta Gorda, Florida, dozens of golf balls fell from the sky. No local golf courses reported missing any balls. Reporters covering the story offered a theory that a waterspout had sucked up golf balls from a water hazard on a golf course and eventually rained them back down.

Frogs. In 2005, citizens of Odzaci, Serbia witnessed thousands of tiny frogs falling from the sky after a passing storm. The frogs landed safely, then hopped around looking for water. While waterspouts might be the reason, it's hard to fathom they could account for the sheer volume of frogs reported to have fallen, or the fact the amphibians were unharmed by the fall.

Coffee Creamer. Believe it or not, in 1969, the residents of Chester, South Carolina were blanketed with a big, gloppy mess of Cremora mixed with rain. The culprit was easy to mug—the nearby Borden plant. A malfunction in the factory's air vents had sent huge plumes of the powdered mixture into the air, where it was beaten down by the rain into a sloppy white paste.

Russian Booty. For a few glorious minutes in March 2018, an estimated $387 million in gold rained down at Yakutsk Airport. The cargo hatch of the plane carrying the loot ripped off during takeoff, sending nearly 200 bricks of solid gold tumbling on and around the runway.

Boiled Bats. No, that's not a typo. In January 2018, after a heat wave sent temperatures soaring past 111 degrees Farenheit, hundreds of heat-stricken bats fell out of the trees in Campbelltown, Australia. The bats, called flying foxes, can only handle temperatures up to 86 degrees before the heat addles their brains and they basically boil.

Money. I know it's hard to believe, but money falling from the sky has occurred numerous times throughout history. The most recent was an incident over Kuwait City in 2015, when hundreds of thousands of dollars' worth of United Arab Emirates *dirham* currency showered the city.

Spiders. Like something out of a nightmare, an invasion of arachnids have taken over in places such as Australia (2015) and most recently in Brazil (2019). The cause wasn't a curse or plague, but a natural act called "ballooning." Ballooning is the term for when spiders produce filaments and launch themselves into the air in order to travel to new horizons. While they do this every year, it's highly unusual for so many spiders to do it at the same time, as they did in the "mass ballooning" invasions mentioned above.

Fish. Actually, fish are the most common of the "uncommon rains." Fish subject to being sucked up by waterspouts on lakes and in oceans, then deposited inland. "Fish rain" has been documented everywhere from Australia to Mexico. The latest case reported was in 2017. To some, the fish from heaven are seen as a blessing. One small village in Honduras, Yoro, even celebrates the "*lluvia de peces*," or "rain of fish" at least once a year.

Fun Fact: Speaking of unnatural rain, keep an eye out for Tiangog-1. The model space station is currently decaying and falling to Earth. But don't fret. Your odds of winning the Powerball lottery are a million times greater than getting struck by falling space debris.

Hey! You Got a License for that Tutti-Frutti?

You've heard the term tutti-frutti, right? Most likely, it triggers memories of the song *Tutti Frutti*, written by Little Richard and Dorothy LaBostrie.

First recorded in 1955, the catchy tune went on to become a massive hit for Little Richard. (I bet you're singing it right now in your head. Am I right?) That's a testament to how popular the song was. But what exactly is tutti-frutti, and where did it originate?

Actually, it's Italian. Tutti means "all," and frutto—as you may have already guessed—means "fruit." Frutti is the plural of frutto, so put them together and tutti-frutti means, "all fruits."

In Italy, tutti-frutti is the name of a colorful confectionery containing candied fruits and nuts. It's also the name of a fruity ice cream.

In the Netherlands, tutti-frutti is a compote of dried fruits. In Luxembourg, it's canned fruit cocktail. In Belgium, it's a dessert of raisins, prunes, apricots, dates, and figs. In the US, we take our tutti-frutti a bit more seriously, usually soaking the fruit in brandy or fermenting it for a nice alcoholic punch.

Tutti-frutti has been around quite a while. One of the first recorded uses of the term appeared on a dinner bill in England dated 1860. It was also one of the first gum flavors sold in vending machines. (The Adams New York Gum Company introduced it in 1888.) That makes tutti-frutti at least 163 years old.

Even so, until recently, no one saw the need to lay claim to the name. But on April 18, 2008, ILTF, Inc. filed for a trademark. The term Tutti-Frutti was awarded to the company on July 13, 2010, for, among other things; carry-out and express restaurant services featuring frozen yogurt and frozen yogurt-based desserts.

Trademarking the names of foods seems to be a growing trend. Here are a few you may or may not have heard of:

Slyder. In 1994, White Castle was granted a US trademark for "Slyder," a variant on slider, derived from the way their burgers slide out of their cardboard cartons.

Double-Double. If you're an In-N-Out burger fan, it may surprise you to know that in 2008, the chain trademarked "Double-Double" as "a sandwich, namely, a burger, the principle ingredients of which are two meat patties and two slices of cheese."

Fonut. In 2011, pastry chef Waylynn Lucas and her partner, voice actor Nancy Truman, trademarked the term "Fonut" for their signature "faux doughnut" that is baked instead of fried.

Crunchburger. Celebrity chef Bobby Flay made a practice of adding a handful of potato chips between the meat patty and the top bun on his famous gourmet burgers. He called it a "Crunchburger." In 2008, his company was awarded a trademark for the term. Flay said, "We didn't invent it, but we *did* trademark it."

Cronut. The brainchild of Dominique Ansel, the Cronut is a crossbreed between a doughnut and a croissant. Deep fried and filled with seasonal pastry creams, lines form at his SoHo bakery daily. The term "Cronut" was registered with the US Patent and Trademark Office in 2015.

Fun Fact: Good thing the tutti-frutti trademark didn't apply to song lyrics! Since Little Richard's song topped the charts in 1955, a few other artists have taken a stab at hitting gold with *Tutti Frutti*, his fun dance hit. (All this despite the fact that the lyrics, while fun to sing, for the most part make no sense.)

Who gave it a shot? Take a look. I think you'll be surprised!

⬥ Pat Boone (1956)

⬥ Elvis (1957)

⬥ MC5 (1970)

⬥ Gene Okerlund (1985)

◈ The California Raisins (1988) (Remember the TV commercials?)

◈ Queen (1992)

Don't Have a Cow, Snooty!

Living in Florida, I'm privileged to get to see one of the rarest mammals on the planet ... *manatees*.

The gentle sea cows are easiest to spot in the winter. Why? Because even though an adult can weigh up to 1200 pounds and grow to between 9 and 10 feet long, they still get cold! (Like most of us native Floridians. LOL.) Once water temperatures dip below 68%, manatees begin congregating to bask in warmer, shallower waters along the shorelines.

One of their favorite winter hangouts is the warm water in the discharge canal of Big Bend power plant in Apollo Beach, Florida. It's become such a refuge that it's been designated by the state and Federal governments as a "manatee sanctuary." The site even sports a 50-foot observation tower to allow human visitors to watch the sea cows basking in their unintentional man-made spa.

Once you get a good look at them, it's hard to believe that old-time sailors mistook manatees for mermaids. (Perhaps not seeing a woman for months or even years had something to do with it.) But did you know manatees even fooled Christopher Columbus himself? In a ship log dated January 9, 1493, he wrote,

> "...*distinctly saw three mermaids, which rose well out of the sea; but they are not so beautiful as they are said to be, for their faces had some masculine traits.*"

No kidding, Chris. It's hard to win a beauty contest when you've got whiskers and there's an elephant swimming around in your gene pool. That's right. The manatee's closest living relative is *the elephant*.

As close cousins, elephants and manatees share some interesting characteristics, such as:

◇ Leathery, grey skin.

◇ Just two nipples, located near the "armpits" of their front legs/ flippers.

◇ Prehensile mouth parts. The elephant has its flexible trunk. The manatee has a flexible upper lip that's split into left and right sides that can move independently. Manatees use their prehensile lips to forage for food and for social interaction.

◇ Continuously replaceable teeth. Throughout their entire lives, new teeth grow in at the rear as older teeth fall out, pushing the teeth forward like a slow conveyor belt.

◇ Hearts that are rounded on the bottom. (Unlike all other animals, whose hearts come to a point. Including humans.)

◇ Membership in the *sirenian* group. This class of animals includes manatees, dugongs, elephants, mastodons, and wooly mammoths.

◇ Size. Manatees are the ocean's largest herbivores. Elephants are the largest *land* herbivores.

There are three species of manatees. All of them possess no incisors or canine teeth—just four rows of molar-like teeth in their cheeks. They live along marshy coastal waters and rivers in the Caribbean, western Africa, and the Amazon River. Other fascinating facts about manatees include:

◇ They can live in freshwater and salt water. (In salt water, they need to find a source of fresh water to drink, like a spring. But a water hose at a boat dock will do. They'll chew right through it to catch a sip!)

◇ Manatees typically surface every three to five minutes to breathe, and can replace 90% of the air in their lungs with a single breath. (We humans can only replace about 10% per breath.)

◇ They can hold their breath underwater for 15 to 20 minutes at a time.

◈ Their eyes close in a circular motion, like a camera aperture.

◈ Manatees are nearsighted and can only see colors in the blue, green, and gray spectrum.

◈ They can eat a tenth of their body weight a day. (They eat around 60 types of fresh and saltwater plants.)

◈ They sleep for up to 12 hours a day.

◈ Manatees have no natural predators. Their main threats are red tide and boats. (Up to 97% of Florida manatees bear scars from boat collisions.)

◈ They live on average for 40 years, but can live as long as 60 years or more.

◈ They swim at an average pace of five mph, but can swim in bursts up to 20 mph.

◈ Manatees can give birth every two years. Usually they deliver one calf weighing up to 66 pounds after a year-long gestation period.

◈ They use their flippers to "walk" along the bottom surface and dig for plants and roots.

◈ Manatees play by barrel-rolling and body surfing.

Oh, and one more thing. Manatees have the smallest brains of all mammals in relation to their body mass. But don't call them stupid! According to studies, manatees possess good long-term memories, and they demonstrate discrimination and task-learning abilities similar to dolphins. So, manatees may not be mermaid-pretty, but they sure aren't dumb.

Fun Fact: The oldest manatee on record was named Snooty. One of the first recorded captive manatee births, he was born at the Miami Aquarium and Tackle Company on July 21, 1948. Never in the wild, Snooty became one of the few manatees in the US allowed to interact with human handlers. As such, Snooty taught us a lot about his species before he passed away two days after his 69th birthday.

Now That's a Real Snow Job

Feeling a little chilly? We've all heard stories about how our grandparents had to walk 30 miles in a blizzard to get to school every day. Whether they were telling the truth or spinning tall tales, there's no denying the storms listed below were real. They're the worst in US recorded history ... to date.

1. *The Great White Hurricane*. This storm hit the Northeast in March of 1888 and left over 4.5 feet (55 inches) of snowfall in some areas. Major cities like Boston and New York City froze to a stop as the snow buried and destroyed railway tracks and telegraph lines. The storm raged on for three days, killing 400 people and inspiring Boston to build the country's first underground subway system.

2. *The Knickerbocker Storm*. More than two feet of snow descended on Washington, D.C. on one fateful day—January 28, 1922. The sheer weight of it collapsed the roof of the Knickerbocker Theatre, killing 98 people. To date, this storm still holds the record for most snowfall in D.C., and the theatre collapse is still the city's deadliest disaster.

3. *The Great Appalachian Storm*. Over Thanksgiving weekend in 1950, this storm literally blasted through the central Appalachians, dumping over five feet of snow (62 inches) in many areas. After the storm passed, temperatures rose to unseasonably warm temperatures, melting the snow and causing extensive flooding blamed for at least 160 deaths.

4. *The Blizzard of 1978*. While this storm doesn't have an impressive name, it delivered some devastating damage. The nor'easter struck on February 5, dumping record snowfall in Boston (27.1 inches), Providence (27.6 inches) and Atlantic City (20.1 inches). The unexpected veracity of the storm's hurricane winds and coastal flooding caught thousands unaware, forcing them to shelter in place for days, or remain trapped in their vehicles on snowed-over roadways. An estimated 100 died as a result.

5. *The Storm of the Century*. In March of 1993, new-fangled technology in the form of a computer forecast model predicted that a storm would hit the East

Coast. Little did they know it would stretch from as far south as Georgia all the way north to Maine. Powerful wind gusts and frigid temperature drops resulted in massive snowfall of up to five feet (60 inches) in some areas. At one point, every major airport on the East Coast had to shut down. While the warnings saved lives, 318 people still perished in the deadly storm.

6. *The Great Blizzard of 2003.* Striking on Valentine's Day and raging for five days, this hellish storm swept across the Mid-Atlantic and Northeast, killing 27 as it dumped a two-foot blanket of snow on every major city from Boston to Washington, D.C. Airports suspended flights and ceased operations. Busy metropolises like Boston and New York City became icy ghost towns as residents hunkered down to stave off the cold.

7. *Snowmageddon.* Depending on who you ask, Snowmageddon refers to the storm that hit on February 4-7, 2010, or to both it *and* the double-punch storm that followed just two days later on February 9-11. Together, the two wreaked icy havoc across the entire nation, shutting down the federal government in D.C. and icing over roads in New Mexico. Massive power outages and transportation shutdowns led to the deaths of 41 people in the US and Mexico.

8. *Snowzilla.* Yet another monster of a storm struck in January 2016. Paralyzing the entire East Coast, it dumped snow as far south as the Florida Panhandle. The worst hit was Glengary, West Virginia, at 42 inches. Snowfall, hail, and wind gusts created whiteout conditions, making travel unsafe for even short distances. Hundreds of thousands of residences lost power, and 55 people lost their lives.

Fun Fact: You might think Florida would be immune to winter hazards, but you'd be wrong. During the rare times temperatures dip into the 40s or below, weather reports from Tampa southward begin broadcasting an unusual warning: Watch out for falling iguanas. Yes, *falling iguanas.*

The tree-climbing reptiles aren't native to Florida. Yet so many have found their way to the Sunshine State inside visitors' luggage, by escaping kids' terrariums, or by surviving pet stores destroyed by hurricanes, that they now roam free there in the thousands. The trouble is, when it gets too cold outside, iguanas kind of freeze up. Once immobilized, the green reptiles lose their grips on their tree perches and tumble down like miniature Grinches, ready to knock you out and steal your Christmas cheer. Bah, humbug!

Feeling Lucky, Punk?

Whenever I daydream about winning the lottery, that country song *Take this Job and Shove It* starts playing in my mind. The singer who made the tune famous in 1977 is named Johnny Paycheck. Gotta love the irony, eh?

So, what would you do if you won big bucks playing the lottery? Here are some interesting stats you might find hard to believe.

⬦ Nearly half (48%) of lottery winners keep working after they win!

⬦ The average American spends $218 a year on lottery tickets.

⬦ The largest US lottery jackpot win was $1.59 billion in 2016—from a $2 Powerball ticket!

⬦ In 2009, 11 states generated more revenue selling lottery tickets than from collecting their citizens' income taxes.

⬦ Roughly 37,000 people have become millionaires playing scratch tickets.

⬦ Lottery statistics from 2022 suggest the chances of winning Mega Millions is one in 302.6 million.

⬦ You're 1,100 times more likely to die over the weekend (between Friday and Monday) than to win the lottery.

⬦ Including all causes of death, the only one less likely to happen than winning the lottery is to be struck by lightning.

⬦ As of March 2022, Powerball was being sold in 48 US lotteries. The chances of winning the jackpot are 1 in 292.5 million.

⬦ In the US, the lottery is played the most by people aged 45-54.

◈ As of May 2021 statistics, your lottery payout will likely shrink by 24-37% after Uncle Sam takes his cut of federal and state taxes.

◈ Within a few years of winning, between 44% and 70% of lottery winners are broke. The main reason? Generosity. They try to help too many people with their cash bonanza.

Fun Facts: The first recorded instance of a lottery (keno slips) comes from China. They're dated from between 201 and 187 BC. Today, people spend more money playing the lottery than on any other form of entertainment. In 2014, Americans shelled out over 70 billion on lottery tickets. That's more money than they spent on sports tickets, video games, books, movie tickets, and music *combined*!

Death on the Menu

I don't know about you, but when it's my time to go, I want to be asleep in a nice, warm bed after spending the day laughing with friends and eating my fill of fried bacon and gooey brownies.

While even prisoners on death row are allowed to indulge in a last meal before they expire, here are seven kinds of food-related deaths the victims never saw coming:

1. **Corks.** On average, an astounding 24 people are killed by champagne corks every year.

2. **Chocolate.** According to Russian news reports, in 2016 a 24-year-old woman died after falling into a vat of molten chocolate at a confectionery factory. Accounts differ, but Svetlana Roslina met her fate either trying to retrieve her dropped cellphone or while adding flour to the mixture.

3. **Soup.** In 2012, an 88-year-old Brazilian woman went to a hospital in Rio de Janiero after suffering a stroke. While under hospital care, Ilda Vitor Maciel died of a pulmonary embolism after hospital workers injected soup into her intravenously instead of into her feeding tube.

4. **Soggy Buns.** Throughout the ages, the accounts of royal gluttony are pretty spectacular. But Adolf Frederick, the king of Sweden in the 1700s, set a new bar by eating himself to death at a single sitting. In 1771, he died after consuming a humongous meal that included caviar, seafood, sauerkraut, and 14 buns soaked in warm milk. What a way to go!

5. **Coconuts.** Believe it or not, around 150 people a year die from being hit by coconuts falling from palm trees.

6. **Beer.** During the London Beer Flood of 1814, eight people were killed when 135,000 gallons of ale burst out of the Meux and Company Brewery.

7. **Carrots.** After drinking 10 gallons of juice in 10 days, Basil Brown died due to an overdose of Vitamin A and severe liver damage. What's up with that, doc?

Fun Fact: An Austrian burgher named Hans Steininger went down in history for two things—having the longest beard in the world (4.5 feet long) and meeting his death because of it.

For convenience, Steininger usually kept his beard rolled up in a leather pouch under his chin. But when a fire broke out at his house in 1567, he neglected to stow it away properly. As a result, he tripped on his beard as he fled. Some say he broke his neck in the fall. Others report he burned to death. But by all accounts, Steininger's beard was the cause of both his rise to fame—and his ultimate downfall.

What Planet are You From, Anyway?

With Elon Musk and his company SpaceX planning a trip to Mars around 2029, it appears it won't be long before interplanetary space travel becomes an actual thing. Who knew?

But if you don't want to wait until then, you don't have to. You can visit every single planet in our solar system by car, right in the good old US of A. (And it doesn't have to be a flying car like George Jetson's.)

Ready to roll? Okay! Tank up and start your engine. We're about to take off on a tour that's (sort of) out of this world ...

First stop is the sun. Sixteen miles northwest of downtown Phoenix, Arizona, you'll find *Sun City*. Established as a retirement community in 1960, it started out with five model homes, a shopping center, a rec center, and a golf course. By 2020, the *Sun*'s inhabitants had grown to around 40,000.

Departing *Sun City*, Arizona, head 342 miles northwest to *Mercury*, Nevada. Named back in the 1850s for the mercury-rich ores mined in the Calico Hills in the region, *Mercury* started out simply as the name of the dusty road that lead to the mines. But in the 1950s, military housing was built there. *Mercury* soon became a town, complete with post office, movie theater, bowling alley—and atomic bombs. Yes, you read that right. From 1951-1962, *Mercury* was an atomic testing site. Today, it's largely a restricted area, so unless you're military, you can only do a drive-by.

From *Mercury*, hang a U-turn and head southeast toward Texas. (The distance between *Mercury* and *Venus* is a spooky 1,111 miles.) Before the 1880s, *Venus* was known simply as "Gossip." Then a man named J.C. Smythe bought 80 acres and planned a town-site. He named it after a local doctor's daughter, Venus. Since then, the tiny town has been included in three Hollywood films. *Bonnie and Clyde* (1967), *The Trip to Bountiful* (1985), and *Born on the Fourth of July* (1989).

Next stop: *Earth*. It's in Texas, too. From *Venus*, take 1-20 west 406 miles to Lamb County. There you'll find the one and only *Earth*, USA. One story credits a resident named O.H. Reeves for naming the place in the 1920s. Actually, he named it *Good Earth* due to the area's fertile soil. When the post office came in 1925, the name got shortened to plain old *Earth*.

Okay, prepare to blast off from *Earth* toward *Mars*. Unlike Elon Musk, it won't take seven months to get there. (Unless you're traveling in a clunker.) Just get on I-44 eastbound, hit warp drive, and travel 1,462 miles to *Mars*, Pennsylvania. This town got its start when Samuel Parks built a house there in 1873 and established the *Mars* post office inside his home. Unlike some of the other "planets" on our tour, *Mars*, PA embraces its name. They've got alien figures scattered around town and a giant flying saucer at the town's center. (Current "Martian" population: 1,600.)

Like an intergalactic snowbird, head south to Florida for our next planet, *Jupiter*. Located in Palm Beach County, get set for a trek of 1,117 miles nearly due south. How did *Jupiter* get its odd moniker? Early Spanish explorers named a local river the Rio Jobe after the Hobe Indian tribe in the region. Later, the name was mistakenly transcribed as Jove. When Spain ceded Florida to Britain, Jove (the Roman name for the Greek god Zeus, who was identical to Jupiter) was anglicized to *Jupiter*.

Our trip around the solar system next takes us back to Texas on our way to *Saturn*. From *Jupiter*, FL head north on I-75 and hang a left in Lake City onto I-10, westbound. From here, its a 1,230 mile road trip to the sixth rock from the sun, *Saturn*. The Texas town was first known as Possum Trot, then Prickly Pear, then Ettowa before finally settling on *Saturn* in 1902. Why *Saturn*? Because back then, Federal guidelines required new post offices to use short town names of only one or two syllables. Local folks submitted the names Mars, Saturn, Jupiter, Apollo, and Io for consideration. Postal authorities picked, well, you know who.

Our next spot, *Uranus*, isn't actually a town. It's more like an unincorporated tourist spot along historic Route 66 in Pulaski County, Missouri. You'll find it 767 miles up I-44 E, north bound from *Saturn*. The area boasts several businesses, a museum, a restaurant, and a water tower. It even briefly had its own newspaper in 2018—The *Uranus Examiner*. (No guide to the planets would be complete without a joke about Uranus, right? But there really *was* a *Uranus Examiner*!)

Shooting out of **Uranus** onto I-44, travel 501 miles east/northeast to **Neptune**, Ohio. This place was established in 1837 by William Bonafield. He laid out the unincorporated town and called it **Neptune**, the Roman god of freshwater and the sea. He may have been inspired by nearby construction that began that same year on a man-made lake. The largest one in the world at the time, it's now known as Grand Lake St. Mary's.

Is our tour done? That depends. Is **Pluto** really a planet or just a dwarf planet? I wish those scientist folks would make up their minds!

For sake of argument (and to continue the fun), let's say a dwarf planet is *still* a planet, and head to **Pluto**, Mississippi. Okay, from **Neptune**, Ohio, head south on I-40 W for 773 miles to **Pluto**. Home to cotton fields and cypress swamps, don't blink or you might miss it. (The town of **Pluto** is even tinier than the planet!) So, why was it named **Pluto**? Accounts vary, but some say it got its moniker from the Lord of the Underworld, because **Pluto** is mostly just one big, hellish swamp.

So, there you go! You've made a complete trip around the solar system, and you didn't even have to get up off your keister. Take *that*, Elon Musk!

Fun Fact: Planets aren't the only weird places to visit in America. Across the US, there are all kinds of towns with crazy names. Here are few to tickle your funny bone:

◇ Two Egg, Florida

◇ Okay, Oklahoma

◇ George, Washington

◇ Scratch Ankle, Alabama

◈ Santa Claus, Indiana

◈ Fries, Virginia

◈ Dinosaur, Colorado

◈ American Fork, Utah

◈ Truth or Consequences, New Mexico

◈ Whynot, North Carolina

That's My Story and I'm Sticking to It

Couples are always being asked how they met. There's even a term for it—the "meet cute." But what if the way you met wasn't so cute?

For some people, it's more of a collision than a meeting. But I guess it doesn't really matter. When the universe brings two people together, there's no stopping it. Check out these weird ways couples claim to have met:

- Running for cover during a drive-by shooting.
- When his dog got her dog pregnant.
- During a pizza delivery.
- Killing a bug on a school locker.
- Wrongly receiving each other's mail.
- Being introduced by an ex-spouse.
- Cleaning a public pool shut down after someone pooped in it.
- Working on a cadaver at med school.
- While training her at Walmart.
- When showing off his six-toed foot.
- Complaining to each other about their bad boss.
- While riding a rollercoaster.
- Washing clothes at a laundromat.
- At a Halloween costume parade for dogs.
- At a Star Wars beer tasting.
- Moving into the apartment he was moving out of.

Fun Facts: Not all meet-cutes turn into marriages. Here are some interesting facts on sticking together:

- The longest marriage on record is between Herbert and Zelmyra Fisher from the US. The couple had been married for 86 years and 290 days when Mr. Fisher passed away in 2011.
- The shortest marriage on record is 55 hours—between Britney Spears and Jason Alexander.
- According to the UN, the country with the highest divorce rate is the

Maldives, with 11 divorces per 1,000 inhabitants. Next up is Belarus, with 4.63 divorces per thousand. US comes in third at 4.34 out of 1,000 calling it splitsville.

It's Raining Gems, Halleluiah!

If there were people living on Uranus, they'd be the butt of every joke in the solar system, right? I mean, seriously, tell me didn't you just picture tiny little people living on your ... well, you know where.

Then again, if you were actually *from Uranus*, you probably wouldn't give a fig about being made fun of. In fact, you'd probably be laughing along with the crowd—all the way to the bank.

Why? Because on Uranus, it rains *diamonds*.

What?!?!

We mere Earthlings go nuts for those shiny, clear rocks because of their beauty and scarcity. (And, of course, because of all those radio and TV commercials that tell us to.) On our planet, it takes millions—even *billions*—of years for diamonds to form. And when they do, it's only deep within the Earth's core.

You see, diamonds only make it to Earth's surface by being belched out of erupting volcanoes. But while diamonds are a rarity here, scientists believe they could be as plentiful on other planets as ... well ... *rain*.

How could that be? First off, we need to know how diamonds are formed. It's pretty simple, really. Diamonds are a simple mixture of hydrogen and carbon molecules that get squeezed together at incredible pressure until they crystalize. While this takes eons on Earth, it could, theoretically, happen *instantly* on other planets.

Research shows that ice giants like Neptune and Uranus have incredible levels of atmospheric pressure that could result in precipitating rain in the form of diamonds, according to scientists from the US Department of Energy's SLAC National Accelerator Laboratory. (How'd you like to have to have to say *that* on your answering machine?)

While the pressure needed to form diamonds is thought to exist 5,000 miles below the surface of these ice giants, the discovery of the presence of oxygen on

Neptune and Uranus makes diamond formation a possibility in a wider range of conditions—quite possibly even as diamond rain.

In an experiment conducted in 2017, these same scientists from that long-named lab above simulated the environment found inside Neptune and Uranus, and were able to create and observe diamond rain for the first time! So, who knows? In a hundred years, we might be saying "Uranus is a girl's best friend."

Fun Fact: Okay, I couldn't resist. Here's what I consider to be the penultimate Uranus joke:

What do Charmin bath tissue and the Star Ship Enterprise have in common?

They both circle Uranus in search of Klingons.

I'll show myself out ...

Write When You Get a Job

Boss a jerk? Hate your boring 9 to 5? Wishing for a more challenging, rewarding career? Here are some options I bet never crossed your mind—but they may be right up your alley:

Fake Mourner. Let's face it. Not everybody has a load of friends standing by to attend their funeral. And if you live long enough, they may all be gone when you finally kick the bucket yourself. What's an unlucky stiff to do? When budgeting for burial services, throw in a few extra bucks for some fake mourners. Don't laugh. (Well, at least not at the funeral.) You can make $50 bucks or more to stand around a coffin and look sad. Plus, lots of times there are free snacks!

Chicken Sexer. No, this job isn't about getting laid. It's about being able to tell the difference between male and female fluffy little chicks. For obvious reasons, egg producers need only female chicks to add to their stocks of laying hens. That's where you come in. As a full-time chicken sexer, on average you'll get a close-up look at about a million chick-butts a year. Typical annual salary is $22,480, give or take a cluck.

Snake Milker. Snake venom is in big demand for the production of anti-venom, and for use in medical research. Job duties entail catching the venomous snakes (in their cages, whew!). Then you have to pry open their jaws and make them sink their fangs into the edge of a cloth-topped container. Why? To release the venom for collection. A true professional can milk 1,000 snakes a week or more. Open positions are scarce, but if you slither into one, you can expect to make around $30,000 a year.

Odor Judge. This position requires workers to smell-test new products and formulas for aroma and/or effectiveness. Duties range from lab-testing products' chemical compositions to taking odiferous whiffs of smelly feet and armpits. Usually a bachelor's degree in chemistry is required. Still, the salary is nothing to sniff at. You can typically earn between $37,500 and $82,500 annually. But ultimately, only you can judge whether it's worth it or not.

Pet Food Tester. It's a dog-eat-dogfood world out there—if you're a "Food Technologist," that is. Your job is to sample Fido's food and make sure it has the right texture, taste, and mouth feel to deliver that delicious appeal pets crave. (While a dog might not care a whit about it, we all know cats can be downright persnickety, right?) The job usually requires a background in Food Science and pays upwards of $40,000 a year. Hot dog!

Legal Bank Robber. Fancy doing the crime, but not doing the time? You might consider becoming a "Penetration Tester." As one, you'd get paid to test the levels of security at banks and other establishments. Of course, if your IT skills are bigger than your biceps, you could find work legally testing computer security systems by attempting to hack them, steal identities, or trick phone operators out of giving up customer details. The average starting salary in the US is over $100,000. Experienced PTs can bring in $160,000 or more. Hmm. It appears that (anti) crime just might pay after all.

Line Stander. If you've got plenty of patience, this may be the perfect career for you. As the name implies, this job pays you to stand in line for someone who's too busy or just doesn't want to themselves. You could line up for such things as concert tickets, the latest new cellphone, or passes to popular sporting events. Several websites and app services are available to match line standers with paying customers. As of December 2022, the average annual income for a line stander was $42,852 a year. Why not get in line and give it a try?

Drying-Paint Watcher. And you thought *your* job was boring? Some people actually get paid to watch paint dry, keeping an eye out for changes in color and texture. Jobs like these are usually found at paint manufacturing companies and often require a science background. The average salary for a paint watcher in the US in 2022 was $40,371.

Worm Picker. Not for the squeamish, this job has no requirements other than a love of the outdoors and a penchant for getting your hands dirty. The worms you capture can be sold directly to fishermen for bait, or you can contract with fishing stores, labs, and universities to catch, package, and supply worms to them. Entry-level jobs start at around $25,350, with most workers averaging $30,225 a year. (FYI, you can make double that growing your own worms.) As

I write this, there are a lot of "openings" in the trade, with 943 temporary jobs and 134 part-time positions available around the US. Try it—you just might get hooked!

Teddy Bear Surgeon. Sounds a lot nicer than worm picker, doesn't it? And it pays better, too! Formally called a "Teddy Bear Repair Technician," this job requires you to know your way around a needle and thread. Why? Because it's your job to return customers' precious teddy bears to their best state possible. That could entail sewing on eyes, ears, arms and legs, and even removing stains. Every major Build-A-Bear outlet has a technician on staff. You can also open your own Teddy Bear "Hospital" and take on clientele independently. The average salary either way is around $42,350.

Fun Fact: In 2016, Charlie Shackleton wrote, directed, shot and produced an independent experimental film he called, *Paint Drying.* The piece was a protest against film censorship and mandatory classification requirements set by the British Board of Film Classification (BBFC). Shackleton believed their regulations made the cost of independent film making prohibitive in the UK.

Paint Drying consisted of 10 hours and seven minutes of an unchanging view of white paint drying on a brick wall. The BBFC was forced to watch every second of it in order to give the film an age rating classification. *Paint Drying* earned a "U" for Universal, indicating "no material likely to offend or harm." Shackleton raised the 5,936 British pounds needed to pay for the BBFC rating review through a Kickstarter campaign.

Hey, Wise Guy. Fuggedaboutit!

So you want to be a mobster, eh? Sorry, but I can't help you with that. Go ask Louis "Lobster Claw" Langostino, *capish*?

While I can't make you a "Made Man," I *can* help you learn mob lingo. Here are a few terms you may or may not admit to knowing. (I promise I'll never tell. I swear.)

- *Waste Management Business*: a euphemism for organized crime
- *Bagman*: a person designated to collect or distribute illicitly gained moolah
- *Barone*: a landlord
- *Clip*: to murder, axe, whack, hit, burn, pop, ice, put a contract out on, etc.
- *Eat Alone*: to be greedy or keep to one's self
- *Goombah*: a senior member of a criminal gang
- *Juice*: the interest paid to a loan shark
- *Omertà*: to take an oath of silence punishable by death
- *Kick Up*: to give a part of your income to the next up in the command chain
- *A Pass*: a reprieve from being whacked
- *Pay Tribute*: to give the boss a cut of the deal
- *Pinched*: caught by the cops or Feds
- *Made Man*: a member of the mob family
- *Hitting the Mattresses*: going to war with a rival clan or family
- *Rat*: an informant, or someone who snitches or squeals after having been pinched
- *Message Job*: putting a bullet in someone so as to send a message; Through the eye: we're watching you. Through the mouth: you squealed like a rat.
- *The Program*: the witness protection program
- *Button Man*: a hit-man, or someone who's been "made"
- *Cugine*: a young man striving to be made
- *Vig*: the house or bookie's take of gambling profits, or the interest

paid to a loan shark
- *Make One's Bones*: earn credibility by axing someone
- *Spring Cleaning*: hiding, cleaning up, or getting rid of evidence

Fun Facts: Trying to figure out the perfect Mafia moniker for yourself? Here are some real mobster names you can use to draw inspiration from:

- Joseph "Joe Bananas" Bonanno
- Tony "Big Tuna" Accardo
- Luigi "Baby Shanks" Manocchio
- Angelo "Quack Quack" Ruggiero
- Louis "Cock-Eyed Lou" Fratto
- Anthony "Whack Whack" Indelicato
- Israel "Ice Pick Willie" Alderman

10,000 Bedsheets Under the Seas

In 1870, French novelist Jules Gabriel Verne published his classic, *Twenty Thousand Leagues Under the Seas*. (Yes, *Seas,* not Sea.) The story is about an extraordinary voyage into the depths of the unknown aboard the amazing Nautilus submarine commanded by heroic Captain Nemo.

A novel well ahead of its time, Verne's adventure pushed beyond the known boundaries of technology and science. In 1986, 116 years later, another technological marvel similarly pushed the known boundaries—this time of guest hospitality.

It was a hotel under the sea.

Named after the famous author, the place was dubbed the Jules' Undersea Lodge. And 36 years after its construction, it's still the only underwater hotel in the United States. Located in Key Largo, Florida, the Lodge sits on the ocean floor, 30 feet under the waters of the protected "Emerald Lagoon."

The design of the air-conditioned, two-bedroom accommodation is retro-futuristic. Stocked with a TV, CDs and other gadgets from the 1980s and 1990s, the main attractions are three 42-inch-wide round windows. You can relax in front of them and watch the marine life as they swim around and watch you back.

Sounds cool, doesn't it? But there's just one catch. If you want to stay the night inside the lodge you're going to have to learn how to scuba dive. The entrance door is located 21 feet below water.

The brainchild of Dr. Neil Monney and ocean explorer Ian Koblick, the Jules' Undersea Lodge is a full-service hotel. Guests can even opt for a personal chef. At your request, the cook will dive down and prepare a meal for you in your very own cozy kitchen under the sea.

To date, the Jules' Undersea Lodge has hosted more than 10,000 overnight guests. As of 2022, it also enjoyed a 4.5 star rating on Trip Advisor. Sounds like a swimming idea, doesn't it?

Fun Fact: Leave it to my home state of Florida to deliver one of the weirdest jobs imaginable: Scuba-diving pizza delivery man. As if the fact that there's an underwater hotel if Florida isn't quirky enough, Jules' Undersea Lodge also offers 24-hour concierge services. Order your favorite pizza and a frogman will deliver it hot to your underwater door—in a watertight case!

Don't Blame Me. I Wanted to Go to Work...

Hey, there's a reason "work" is a four-letter word. If you're scraping the bottom of the barrel looking for yet another excuse to call in sick, I've got you covered.

Here are some hilarious, hard-to-believe-but-true reasons people gave for missing a day at the office:

- Grandma tried to poison me. *Again.*
- I forgot I was supposed to get married today.
- My cat has the hiccups.
- I was too upset from watching *The Notebook.*
- A deer bit me.
- Someone stole all my daffodils.
- I threw my back out chasing a beaver.
- I thought I'd won the lottery.
- A fox stole my car keys.
- The line was too long at Starbucks.
- My house is haunted.
- I had to go to bingo.
- My son locked me in the trunk of my car.
- I had to audition for *X Factor.*
- A man is coming to hang some pictures.
- I cleaned the house so I wouldn't have to do it after work.
- It's too cold to leave the house. (Okay, I've actually used that one!)
- I visited a farm, petted a pig, and now I have a cold ... or the swine flu. I'm not sure, so I'd better not chance it.
- My plastic surgery needed some "tweaking."
- I had a nightmare and I'm scared to leave the house.
- My goldfish died and I had to bury it.
- I don't want to leave my pet alone.
- I just put a casserole in the oven.
- I saw a UFO so I had to stop and observe it.
- I accidentally washed all my pants at once.
- I woke up in a good mood and I didn't want to ruin it.

Well, at least that *last* one has a ring of truth about it ...

Fun Fact: In actuality, American workers take the least amount of sick time of almost any other nation. But what if you don't work? Or simply don't feel like leaving the house? Here's a few more excuses to keep in your pocket for those special "I-don't-want-to-go" emergencies:

- I accidentally superglued my hand to the fridge door handle, so I'm stuck here.
- I have to redo my online dating profile ASAP.
- I just experienced the death of my soul and I'd appreciate your understanding at this difficult time.
- It's toenail clipping day, so I just don't have the time to spare.
- Darn, I'd love to, but my sister's boyfriend's niece's pet goldfish's baby shower is tonight and I've already committed.

Want a Penn Rose to Go with that Hops Juice?

To paraphrase a line from Shakespeare, "A rose by any other name would still taste like a meat stick."

Wait. What? Okay, before you go Google search it, let me explain. I bet you didn't know it, but *Penn Rose* was the original name chosen for the tasty treat we now know as the *Slim Jim*. (As for the hops juice? Well, that's my silly, made-up name for beer.)

So, how did the Penn Rose become the Slim Jim? It all began in 1929, when a 16-year-old kid dropped out of school in Pennsylvania to become a self-made man.

Apparently undaunted by the hard times of the Great Depression, young Adolph (Al) Levis started out selling pickles, spices, and condiments. Later on, he opened a business in his garage selling pickled pigs' feet, tomatoes, and cabbages to local delis and taverns.

In the 1940s, he partnered with his brother-in-law, Joseph Cherry. Together, they worked with a local meat packer to develop a new kind of dried beef snack that would be just as tasty, yet easier to eat than biting a hunk off a big stick of dried sausage or pepperoni.

Their invention was christened the Penn Rose. (Penn for Pennsylvania, and Rose for Levi's wife Rose.) But the name didn't pass muster with the intended audience—mainly bar patrons. (I mean, who wants to eat a meat flower? Am I right?)

In search of a better name, some say the men took inspiration from the "sophisticated" cigarette brand, Virginia Slims. Besides renaming the product, they packaged the beef sticks in glass jars full of vinegar decorated with a man in a top-hat carrying a cane.

Their clientele were mainly bars. Levis and Cherry hoped the new look and name, Slim Jim, would appear classier and more masculine than Penn Rose had. They were right. Sales of the product took off.

By the 1950s, the Cherry-Levis Food Products company was wrapping individual Slim Jims in cellophane and selling them to bars throughout the Northeast.

In 1967, Levis sold Cherry-Levis to General Mills for around $20 million. In 2021, the Slim Jim brand was ranked #1 in US convenience store sales, with a sales value of $494.5 million. Man, that's a lot of meat sticks!

Fun Fact: The Slim Jim is basically just a stick of dried meat. Now available in 21 different flavors, what makes these tubular treats so popular? In a word—advertising! Here are some he-men who've stepped up to bat for Slim Jims:

> ◈ Professional wrestler Randy Savage, aka "Macho Man." Slim Jim spokesperson from 1993 to 2000, this long-term spokesman would end each commercial by bellowing, "Need a little excitement? Snap into a Slim Jim!"

> ◈ Rapper Vanilla Ice hawked the meat sticks in 2015.

> ◈ Through the years, Slim Jim commercials have featured other wrestlers such as: "The Ultimate Warrior," "Bam Bam Bigelow," "Edge," and Kevin Nash, to name a few.

What's in a Name?

We're all familiar with certain catchphrases, such as "It's all in a day's work." We even use them ourselves. But where did they get their start?

Below are a few interesting ones I had no idea about. Did you?

Winning hands down. This term came from horse racing. A jockey who manages to get far enough ahead can slacken the reins and keep his "hands down."

Jaywalking. The word "*jay*" used to be a term for a greenhorn or a rube—in other words, a foolish, possibly not-too-bright person. In the early 1900s, jay-walker came to describe a person who crossed the street at random, putting themselves and drivers at risk of being injured.

Biting sarcasm. When used deftly, words can feel as sharp as a knife that's drawn blood. So the phrase biting sarcasm is rather fitting, considering the term sarcasm can be traced to the Greek verb "*sarkazein,*" which meant "to tear flesh like a dog."

X as a kiss. If you sign off your letters, texts, or emails with and X as a kiss, you're following a tradition that's hundreds of years old. The first incident can be traced back to a 1736 letter written by British naturalist Gilbert White. (A scholar *and* a romantic, eh?)

Keep calm and carry on. This slogan was originated by the British government during WWII. It was meant to urge citizens to remain civil during air raids deployed by German planes. In the 2000s, it was brought back to life, where the advice seems just as sensible today as it was back then.

Girl. This term for a young female is common today. But back in the 1300s, the word "*gyrle*" used to refer to any young child, whether boy or girl.

Blood-curdling. This slang term has been around since the 1800s, where it was used to describe sensational stories that could "chill the blood." But according to a 2015 study, they may have been on to something way back then.

It's been found that horror movies can actually curdle your blood! Scientists discovered that when we watch something terrifying, our bodies' blood coagulant factor VIII (a clotting protein) goes up. Too much of it in our bloodstream can clot, or "curdle" our blood!

Fun Fact: You probably know her simply as Barbie. But the iconic doll introduced by Mattel, Inc. in March 1959 has a full name. It's Barbara Millicent Roberts. Ruth Handler, who created Barbie, named her after her own daughter, Barbara, who inspired her to design an adult-like doll.

Arizona Vs Alligator

This story is about Arizona Donnie Clark. With a name like that, how could you possibly go wrong? Well, let me tell you, she did. *So* wrong, in fact, that it earned her a place in the history books.

Don't think you've ever heard of her? I bet you have. Read on and find out:

Born in 1873 in Ashgrove, Missouri, Arizona Clark grew up to become one of America's first female mobsters—and one of the most notorious. How bad was she? In the 1930s, the head of the FBI, J. Edgar Hoover himself, described her as "the most vicious, dangerous, and resourceful criminal brain of the last decade."

That was really saying something back then, given that the 1930s were the height of the "public enemy" era—a time when the exploits of criminal gangs made the front-page headlines. But way before any of that happened, at the age of 19, Arizona married a man named George Barker. Over the next decade or so, she bore him four sons.

George worked a variety of low-paying jobs. (An FBI document described his as "shiftless.") To make ends meet, Arizona and her four sons started stealing from the church collection plate. After her brood became adults, they hit the road, terrorizing half the country by committing a string of kidnappings, robberies, and murders.

Their crime spree earned them the name, The Barker-Karpis Gang. Have you figured it out yet? Arizona Donnie Clark was the infamous Ma Barker.

After the Barker clan's streak of criminal mayhem, the FBI was hot on their tails. To avoid capture, Arizona and her boys hid out in Ocklawaha, Florida, in a two-story cracker house they rented on Lake Weir. Little did they know that the lake was also home to Gator Joe, a huge alligator with a reputation almost as notorious as the Barkers themselves.

Gator Joe was a local legend in Ocklawaha long before the Barkers arrived. Though the Barkers tried to shoot and kill Gator Joe on many occasions, they never could.

Ironically, all that gunfire and ruckus caught the attention of people out trying to get a look at Gator Joe, and eventually helped lead the FBI to the crooks' hideout. Once the Feds found the Barkers, the longest FBI shoot-out in history commenced.

On January 16th, 1935, Federal agents surrounded the house and shot at it for four solid hours. When the smoke cleared, they discovered that only two Barkers had been home—Arizona and her son Fred. Both were shot dead. According to an FBI account, agents found a Tommy Gun lying in Ma Barker's cold hands.

Is all this true? Some say it isn't. In an effort to make a fair accounting of Arizona, those who knew her insisted that she had played no actual criminal role, but only accompanied her sons on their crime sprees. Reports as of 2022 are consistent in relaying that Arizona's role in her sons' crimes were falsely created by the media to increase newspaper and media sales.

Which accounts are true? Which are false? I'll leave that up to you to decide for yourself.

Fun Fact: Of all the varying accounts, there's one thing we know for sure: Arizona Barker met her demise in Ocklawaha, Florida. But whatever happened to Gator Joe?

Accounts say the creature lived on for a couple more decades, until he crossed paths with a local gator hunter named Vic Skidmore. Skidmore shot Gator Joe dead. When he went to skin him, the gator measured fifteen feet, seven inches. Another tall tale? If you care to, you can check out the gator's foot for yourself. It's still on display at Gator Joe's Beach Bar and Grill in Ocklawaha—right across the street from a little "hole in the wall" called Ma Barker's!

Thank Goodness for Happy Accidents!

Could you imagine life without potato chips? How about without Coca-Cola? No chocolate chip cookies? Say it isn't so!

The world would be a sadder place without these yummy treats, wouldn't it? But if it weren't for a few twists of fate, all three would've likely never been invented. Neither would quite a few of our favorite things. Keep reading and find out who stumbled upon these great ideas, and made history a little tastier with their discoveries:

The Ice Cream Cone. At the St. Louis World's Fair in 1904, an ice cream vendor ran out of dishes to serve his frozen treats in. The man in the cart next to him, Ernest A. Hamwi, just happened to be selling waffles. He came up with the idea to curl his crispy waffles into cones before they hardened. They inserted a scoop of ice cream, and there you have it. The first ice cream cone took shape.

Chocolate Chip Cookies. These delectable treats didn't make their appearance until one fateful day in 1930. That's when Ruth Graves Wakefield, co-owner of the Toll House Inn, realized she was out of baker's chocolate for her chocolate cookies. She decided to chop up a block of Nestle semi-sweet chocolate instead. She thought it would melt and spread evenly in the batter. It didn't. Instead, the chunks remained, well, *chunky*. The new "chocolate chip" cookies were a hit, and they were here to stay!

Popsicles. This frozen treat was invented by an 11-year-old boy named Frank Epperson. He mixed some soda powder with water and left it in the freezer overnight without taking out the stirrer. The next morning, he yanked his frozen soda out of the container by pulling on the stirrer. He then licked it to taste it. Finding it delicious, he called his new concoction the Epsicle. (A combination of Epperson and icicle.) Years later, his kids kept referring to his invention as Pop's Sicle. The name, like a tongue on a frozen flagpole, stuck.

Potato Chips. Maybe it's just me, but I find it amusing that the guy who invented potato chips was named George Crum. Anyway, in 1953 Crum was working as a chef at the Moon Lake Lodge Resort in Saratoga Lake, NY. One day, a customer complained about the French fries being soggy. To appease them, Crum cut the potatoes into thin slices and fried them until they were crispy brown chips. Ta-da! A snack-food legend was born.

Coca-Cola. The guy who created the syrup for this iconic beverage wasn't a chef—he was a pharmacist. In 1886, Dr. John Stith Pemberton was trying to create a way to wean addicts off morphine and other drugs by creating an alcoholic drink containing cocaine and caffeine. He dubbed his concoction Coca-Cola. (When Prohibition hit, Pemberton was forced to remove the alcohol from his formula, but the cocaine remained until about 1903.) Today, the drugs are gone, but the caffeine and fizz live on. Coca-Cola is still the #1 selling brand of carbonated beverage in the world.

Fun Fact: Another happy accident involves the discovery of chewing gum. In the late 1800s, American inventor Thomas Adams, Sr. stumbled upon the chewy treat while he was trying to turn chicle (the stuff gum is made out of) into rubber.

In 1848, quite on purpose, John B. Curtis developed and sold the first commercial chewing gum. Called The State of Maine Pure Spruce Gum, he got the idea from American Indians who regularly chewed resin made from the sap of spruce trees.

The Heavenly Hairdresser

If your hair is anything like mine, making it look good requires a hairdresser who is part artist, part miracle-worker, and part saint. You need someone like Pierre Toussaint. His life story—just like his coiffure skills—is nothing short of miraculous. Read on and decide for yourself:

On June 28, 1766, Pierre was born into slavery in Haiti on a plantation owned by the Bérard family. Raised as a Catholic, he was educated by the Bérard's tutors and trained to be a house slave. In 1797, Haiti experienced a growing rebellion by Haitian slaves and free people of color. Fearing for their lives, the Bérards left for New York City, taking Pierre and four other slaves with them.

Upon their arrival in New York, the Bérards had Pierre apprentice at one of the city's leading hairdressers, allowing him to keep most of his earnings. When Mr. Bérard died, Pierre voluntarily took on the support of Madame Bérard. She eventually remarried, but on her deathbed in 1807, she made her new husband promise to free Pierre.

True to his word, her husband did. Pierre was made a free man. As such, he chose the last name "Toussaint," in honor of General Toussaint Louverture, the hero of the Haitian Revolution. The name turned out to be a rather apropos moniker, as Pierre was about to start a kind of revolution of his own ...

Toussaint quickly became a highly successful barber among New York's upper echelon. As a result, he made a very good living. One of the first things he did with his money was to pay for his sister Rosalie's freedom.

After that, Toussaint began putting his wealth to good use supporting various philanthropic causes. One of them was help in financing the construction of Old St. Patrick's Cathedral. Toussaint is also credited as the de facto founder of Catholic Charities in New York.

In 1811, Toussaint married Juliette Noel after purchasing her freedom. Together they began a career of charity, often taking baked goods to children at the Orphan Asylum and donating money toward its operations. The couple also sheltered orphans and fostered numerous boys, supporting them in getting an education and learning a trade.

They created a credit bureau, an employment agency, and a refuge for priests and needy travelers. (Many Haitian refugees went to New York. Because Toussaint spoke both French and English, he frequently helped them.) In addition, during an epidemic, Toussaint was "renowned for crossing barricades to nurse quarantined cholera patients."

Rather saintly of him, wouldn't you say? A few other folks thought so, too. Upon his death in 1853 at the age of 87, Toussaint was the first and only layman to be buried in the crypt below the main altar of the Saint Patrick's Cathedral on Fifth Avenue. (It's generally reserved for bishops and the Archdiocese of New York.)

In the 1950s, the John Boyle O'Reilly Committee for Interracial Justice (devoted to social justice for blacks), began researching and publicizing Toussaint's life story. Because of his reputation of great charity, Cardinal Terence Cooke, the then Archbishop of New York, authorized a canonization committee to study Toussaint's life further. (As part of it, Cardinal John O'Connor had Toussaint's body exhumed and examined.)

On December 17, 1997, Toussaint was declared "Venerable" by Pope John Paul II. This step puts Toussaint, a man committed to serving others, firmly on the road to become North America's first black saint.

Fun Fact: Boston stakes the claim of hosting the first St. Patrick's Day celebration in America. On March 17, 1737, two dozen Irish immigrants gathered to honor St. Patrick and to establish the Charitable Irish Society. The oldest Irish organization in the US, it still holds an annual dinner every St. Patrick's Day.

That's all well and good, but hold my green beer for a second ...

Evidence was recently unearthed in St. Augustine, Florida that may rewrite the history books. While studying Spanish gunpowder expenditure logs, historian

Michael Francis (sounds pretty Irish to me) discovered entries that indicate cannon blasts or gunfire were used there to honor St. Patrick way back in 1600.

Records also show that residents of St. Augustine (a Spanish garrison town founded in 1565), congregated and walked down the streets, forming, quite possibly, the first St. Patrick's Day parade—a full *137 years* before Boston. Apparently, one city's about to be green with envy...

The Mother of Invention

The US Patent and Trademark Office opened its doors on July 31, 1790. But it wasn't until May 5, 1809, that the first woman in the US was awarded a patent. Her name was Mary Kies, and her invention was a technique for weaving straw with silk.

She wasn't the first woman to have a brilliant idea, however. You see, before then, many women inventors went completely unacknowledged due to prohibitive laws—or they applied for patents using their husbands' names.

Thankfully times have changed. Even so, today only 10% of US patents are held by women. Still, they've come up with some truly indispensable discoveries. Take a look through this list and discover exactly who invented some of the everyday items you can't live without today:

- *Aquarium*, 1832. Inventor: Jeanne Viilepreux-Power.
- *Bullet-proof fiber*, 1966. Inventor: Stephanie Kwolek.
- *Caller ID and call waiting*, 1970s. Inventor: Shirley Ann Jackson.
- *Car heater*, 1893. Inventor: Margaret A. Wilcox.
- *Central heating*, 1919. Inventor: Alice Parker.
- *Circular saw*, 1812. Inventor: Tabitha Babbitt.
- *Coffee filter*, 1908. Inventor: Melitta Benz.
- *Dishwasher*, 1872. Inventor: Josephine Cochran.
- *Disposable diaper*, 1950. Inventor: Marion Donovan.
- *Electric hot water heater*, 1917. Inventor: Ida Forbes.
- *Electric refrigerator*, 1914. Inventor: Florence Parpart.
- *Fire escape*, 1887. Inventor: Anna Connelly.
- Home security system, 1969. Inventor: Marie Van Brittan Brown.
- *Ice cream maker*, 1843. Inventor: Nancy Johnson.
- *Laser cataract surgery*, 1986. Inventor: Patricia Bath.
- *Life raft*, 1882. Inventor: Maria Beasley.
- *Locomotive chimney*, 1879. Inventor: Mary Walton.
- *Low-reflection glass*, 1935. Inventor: Katharine Blodgett.
- *Medical syringe*, 1899. Inventor: Letitia Geer.

- *Photo enhancement*, 1978. Inventor: Barbara Askins.
- *Retractable dog leash*, 1908. Inventor: Mary A. Delaney.
- *Windshield wiper*, 1903. Inventor: Mary Anderson.
- *Wireless transmission technology*, 1941. Inventor: Hedy Lamarr.
- *Word processor*, 1971. Inventor: Evelyn Berezin.

Fun Facts: Women also helped fuel the space race—literally! In 1957, Mary Sherman Morgan invented Hydyne rocket fuel. In 1974, Yvonne Brill invented a space rocket propulsion system. And in 1980, Olga Gonzalez-Sanabria invented the long-life nickel hydrogen batteries that keep the International Space Station powered up in the dark, when the earth blocks the sun's rays from powering its solar arrays.

If at First You Don't Succeed, Call it Something Else

Hey, not every attempt at making something can be a spot-on success. But sometimes, all you need is a little change in perspective to flip a failure on its head and call it a winner.

Here are some unlikely successes that came from failed attempts, proving there's nothing quite like good-old American ingenuity to turn an onion into a rose:

Silly Putty. During WWII, an engineer named James Wright was given the job of inventing a cheap alternative to synthetic rubber. While working one day, he dropped some boric acid into silicone oil. The result produced a glob of stretchy, bouncy material. When pressed onto newsprint, it also picked up the words and images. He thought it was pretty cool. But his employers, unimpressed, called it "nutty putty."

A few years later, businessman Peter Hodgson saw the potential in Wright's invention. In 1950, his throw-away goop became a smash with kids around the country. Today, over 20,000 plastic eggs full of Silly Putty are sold each and every day.

Post-it Notes. A scientist at 3M named Dr. Spencer Silver was doing research on strong adhesives when he came across a rather wimpy one. It stuck lightly to surfaces, but didn't bond tightly to them. Not having any use for his discovery, it lay about for years until another 3M scientist, Art Fry, came to him with the idea to create a bookmark with it.

After handing the slightly sticky papers around the office, people started asking for more—not to use as bookmarks, but to write notes on. The sticky-note was born. Today, the not-so-wimpy glue is a financial powerhouse for 3M. They currently produce over 50 billion Post-it Notes a year.

Bubble Wrap. While engineers Marc Chavannes and Alfred Fielding invented bubble wrap on purpose, that purpose wasn't for packing material. It was for *wallpaper*! The wallpaper idea flopped. (I never saw *that* coming, did you?)

Undaunted, the pair tried to reinvent their product as greenhouse insulation. That idea fumbled, too.

But in 1960, the idea to use the addictively fun-to-pop sheets of bubbly plastic as material for shipping packages burst into their thoughts. *Voila*! Another product we can't live without had found its true calling. The global market for bubble wrap is projected to be $10.7 billion in 2023.

Matches. In 1826, the best invention since fire itself was discovered by chemist John Walker. Quite by accident, he scraped a stick coated with chemicals across a fireplace hearth. To his surprise, the stick caught fire.

Knowing a good thing when he saw it, Walker started producing his "Friction Lights" using cardboard. Eventually he switched to the wooden sticks and sandpaper strikers we still use today. Let me tell you, that man was on fire! By 2019, the US match industry was producing more than 35 billion matchbooks a year.

Superglue. In 1942, Harry Coover was trying to create materials he could use to build clear, plastic gunsights needed for the war effort. But what he discovered instead was a chemical concoction that stuck to everything it touched. Fellow researchers at Eastman Kodak couldn't see a use for it at the time.

It wasn't until 1951 that a co-worker named Fred Joyner embraced Coover's sticky-wicket of an idea. The formula was patented as "Alcohol-Catalyzed Cyanoacrylate Adhesive Compositions/Superglue." It came on the market in 1958 under the name "Eastman 910," but was shortly thereafter renamed Superglue. Who knew?

Teflon. Today, this synthetic polymer (called PTFE) is used to make a diverse range of things, from nonstick cooking pans to fingernail polish. The scientist who discovered it, Roy J. Plunkett, did so completely by accident while working for DuPont in 1938.

Plunkett was researching refrigerants for air conditioning and refrigeration units when he noticed that some of the gas he was using had turned to white powder. Intrigued, he tested it and found it to be heat-resistant, and to have low surface-friction qualities. You might say the perfect use for it hit him in the head like a frying pan ...

Fun Fact: For over a century now, the US has remained in first place when it comes to being the most inventive nation in the world. During most of that time, Thomas Alva Edison held the title of most prolific American Inventor, racking up an astonishing 1,084 patents between 1869 and 1933.

But in 2015, astrophysicist Lowell Lincoln Wood, Jr. surpassed Edison's record when the US Patent and Trademark Office granted him his 1,085th patent. Aged 74 at the time, Wood was averaging about one new US patent a day! As of 2018, (the latest records I could find) Wood's tally of patents had grown to an astounding 1,761! Makes me wonder who had the brightest bulb after all ...

Bully for the Woolly, Man!

As far as I can tell, only three animals on earth have ever been named woolly. (Besides my hairy cousin Arthur.) One of these creatures, as you probably know, was the woolly mammoth. These huge, ancient relatives of the elephant roamed the cold tundra of Asia, Europe, and North America in hordes until about 10,000 years ago.

They began to die off. But did you know that the last known group of the humongous beasts lived on until around 1650 B.C.? That's over 1,000 years *after* the Pyramids in Egypt were built! (Hmm. Maybe *that's* how they built them—with mammoth power!)

Moving on ... The second animal with woolly in its name is the woolly rhinoceros. It lived alongside the wooly mammoth. But unlike its tusked companion, people who stumbled upon rhino fossils weren't quite sure what to make of them.

Native peoples in Siberia thought the rhino horns were the claws of giant birds. When a skull was found in Austria in 1335, it was believed to belong to a dragon! In 1590, the skull was used as the basis for the head of a statue of a lindworm. (A mythical, giant serpent monster from European folklore.)

That's kind of ironic, considering woolly, by definition, means to be vague and confused, especially when thinking. (Woolly-headed. Woolly-minded.)

Eventually, the woolly rhino's remains were sorted out, and it took its place in the animal record. So, that leaves us with animal number three. Thankfully, it needs no sorting out, because it's still very much alive and with us today.

It's called the *Pyrrharctia isabella*. Or, as you may know it, the isabella tiger moth. Well, actually, that's what it turns into. In its larval stage, it's known as the woolly worm, woolly bear, or the banded woolly bear.

Found in the US and southern Canada, the moth was first formally named by James Edward Smith in 1797. In its woolly stage, the 13-segmented caterpillar larvae are covered with brown hair in their mid-regions and black hair on their front and back areas, making them appear rather like a tiny bear.

So, what makes this woolly little critter so special? Unlike many moths, isabella tiger moths lay their eggs in the fall instead of spring or summer. This means the poor caterpillar larvae must emerge and eat like mad so they can grow the woolly coats they'll need to survive when winter kicks in.

But no matter what the woolly bears do, inevitably, sometime during winter, they end up freezing solid as ice. First their hearts stop beating. Then their guts freeze. Next their blood ices up, followed by the rest of their bodies. But that's okay. In the spring, they thaw out and go on about their business as if nothing happened! How? By producing a special cryoprotectant in their tissues.

Folklore says that the severity of the coming winter can be foretold by the thickness and design of the woolly bears' coats. If the brown midsection is wide, winter weather will be mild. If it's thin, a harsh winter is on its way.

Want to see a woolly bear for yourself? You just might catch a glimpse by attending one of the many woolly bear festivals held every fall. Most feature food, crafts, and woolly bear races. Here's where you'll find them:

- Beattyville, Kentucky
- Little Valley, New York
- Banner Elk, North Carolina
- Vermilion, Ohio
- Oil City, Pennsylvania

Fun Facts: *Wooly Bully* was the name of a 1965 hit song by the novelty rock and roll band, Sam the Sham and the Pharaohs. It was the group's only success, making them a one-hit wonder. What did the term "Wooly Bully" mean? Back then, it was a hip (and somewhat sarcastic) way to congratulate a person. For instance, if someone told you they did something cool, you could say, "Wooly Bully for you." (In other words, "Big deal.")

Thanks, But I Think I'll Pass

Nowadays, advertisers are always vying for our money. In some ways, it's downright scary. Just the other day, I posted a meme about a brand of ice cream, only to see an ad for it pop up as I searched for something on Amazon!

I have to admit, that particular advertiser hit a bullseye by marketing to me. But it doesn't always go so smoothly. Here are a few ads that, well, let's say they didn't quite hit their mark:

Ikea. This Swedish manufacturer thought they'd struck it big when they introduced the "Fartfull Workbench." Fartfull means "full speed" to them, but quite another thing to its English-speaking market in the UK. (Especially after a meal of beans-on-toast.)

Coors. When the American beer company launched its "Turn it Loose" campaign in Spain, they raised quite a stink. You see, the tagline, when translated into Spanish, is a common phrase for having diarrhea.

American Dairy Association. Remember the famous "Got Milk?" campaign? While it was a hit among English speakers in the US, those speaking Spanish wondered by they would be asked, "Are you lactating?"

McDonald's. When the hamburger giant first expanded to France, they brought along their signature "Big Mac." They were about to launch the "Gros Mec" when they discovered the term was French slang for "Big Pimp."

Coca-Cola. As this beverage king expanded its empire into China, it was first read as "Kekoukela," which, depending on the dialect, translates into "bite the wax tadpole," or "female horse stuffed with wax." Scrambling to find a phonetic equivalent, Coca-Cola finally settled on "Kokou kole," which means, "happiness in the mouth."

American Airlines. Wishing to impress flyers with its luxurious leather seats, this international airline came up with the advertising slogan, "Fly in Leather." The Spanish-speaking clientele in Mexico found it rather shocking they would be invited to "Fly Naked."

Parker Pen. When expanding into Mexico, this famous writing instrument company suffered a mix-up while translating the slogan, "It won't leak in your pocket and embarrass you." The Spanish word *embaraza* sounds like embarrass, but it means something entirely different. I wonder how embarrassed Parker executives were when they discovered they'd just told their potential Mexican customers, "It won't leak in your pocket and *impregnate* you."

Mercedes-Benz. In perhaps one of the most spectacular advertising fails of all time, this major automobile manufacturer entered the Chinese market under the brand name, "Bensi." Just one little problem with that. In Chinese, bensi means, "Rush to die." Uh, no thanks...

Fun Fact: As of 2022, the average American is exposed to an astounding 4,000 to 10,000 ads per day!

America's First Bag Lady

Actually, "America's First Lady of Bags" would be a more appropriate moniker for the woman I'm referring to. Who am I talking about? Read on and find out:

Margaret E. Knight was born on Valentine's Day, 1838, in York, Maine. But she was no shrinking violet. As a little girl, "Mattie" shunned dolls, preferring to play with woodworking tools instead. Her family stated that "the only things (she) wanted were a jack knife, a gimlet, and pieces of wood."

As a child, Mattie made kites, sleds, and other toys for her brothers. But the death of her father when she was 12 soon forced Knight to help her mother make ends meet. She took a job at a cotton mill—a notoriously dangerous job at the time.

Soon the young woman witnessed a serious accident caused by a malfunctioning loom. Compelled to help, Knight invented a shuttle restraint system that would become a standard fixture on looms across the nation. Unfortunately, she knew nothing about patenting at the time, and received no compensation for her invention.

That was a mistake Knight would not repeat.

In 1867, she began work at Columbia Paper Bag Company in Springfield, Massachusetts. It didn't take her long to spot ways to improve the manufacturing process. The envelope-like bags being produced were weak, narrow, and couldn't be stood up. That made them poorly suited for bulky items like groceries. Flat-bottomed bags, which were sturdier and more useful, were still being made at the factory by hand, making them expensive to produce.

Knight figured there had to be a way to automate the handwork required. She began tinkering with designing a machine that could feed, cut, and fold the paper automatically, to generate a squared-bottomed bag much like the ones we use today.

Just a year later, her machine was not only designed—it was fully operational. It drastically improved both the output and uniformity of the bags being produced. Knight applied for a patent—but soon realized she was in for a fight.

Charles Annan, a man who worked in the company's machine shop, tried to steal her design. Challenged in court, he argued that Knight didn't design the mechanism herself because she "could not possibly understand the mechanical complexities of the machine."

Annan's accusations forced Knight to spend $100 a day in legal costs for the 16-day hearing. (Over $35,000 in today's dollars.)

Thankfully, she quickly debunked Annan's unsubstantiated claim, showing the court her original blueprints for the machine. She won the case—and the patent. At the time, many female inventors hid their gender by using only initials, but Margaret E. Knight bucked the trend. Her full name is clearly identified on the patent, awarded to her in 1871.

With rights in hand, Knight co-founded her own paper bag company in Hartford, Connecticut called the Eastern Paper Bag Company. Having no desire to run it herself, she opted to receive royalties and to continue to work as an inventor.

Throughout her life, Knight never married, and she never stopped her innovative ways. Before she died in 1914, she'd amassed 25 patents for inventions ranging from a compound rotary engine to a sole-cutting machine for making shoes.

In 2022, Margaret E. Knight was posthumously inducted into the National Inventors Hall of Fame. Not bad for a bag lady, eh?

Fun Facts: The unconventional life of Margaret E. Knight has been celebrated in many ways, including two recent books about her life. If you want to know more about her, check out:

Mattie and the Machine: A Novel. This inspirational young-adult novel was written by Lynn Ng Quezon and published in 2022 by Santa Monica Press.

Marvelous Mattie: How Margaret E. Knight Became an Inventor. This children's book was written by Emily Arnold McCully and published in 2006 by Farrar, Straus and Giroux.

Uh ... Happy Holidays, I Think

In the US, we celebrate the winter holidays in all kinds of ways, from Christmas to Kwanza to Festivus for the rest of us. But around the world, they do things differently. In some cases, *way* differently.

Check out these peculiar holiday traditions from around the world:

Night of the Radishes. Every December 23rd in Oaxaca, Mexico, they celebrate a festival called La Noche de Rabanos. To prepare, artisans and merchants create intricately carved radishes depicting nativity scenes, animals, buildings, and other relevant items. The displays are sold as Christmas centerpieces. But before that, they're judged based on design. The best radish sculpture takes home a monetary prize.

KFC for Christmas. While we're home feasting on turkey and ham, an estimated 3.5 million Japanese families are celebrating Christmas Eve with Colonel Sanders. What? It all started with a marketing stunt in the 1970s called *Kurisumasu ni wa Kentakkii*. (Kentucky for Christmas.) Since then, it's become so popular in Japan that customers pre-order their dinners months in advance.

Lucky Spider Webs. In Ukraine, families decorate their Christmas trees with spider webs. While most of us would find this less than appealing, to say the least, for Ukrainians, spider webs are associated with good fortune. Why? It's all due to an old story about a poor family who grew a Christmas tree from a pine cone. The children wanted to decorate it, but they couldn't afford to. So spiders came to the rescue! They spun webs around the tree that turned silver and gold in the sunlight, giving the family a beautifully adorned tree. And the rest is spider-web history ...

The Pooping Log. (No, that's not a typo.) The Spanish region of Catalonia has quite a unique and wacky holiday tradition called *Tió de Nadal*. Roughly translated, it means Christmas Log. But not just any old log. This is a limb that's been hollowed-out and given a face, legs, and a little red hat.

Beginning each December 8th, families "feed" the log with presents and candy each night. They also put a blanket of it to keep it warm. On Christmas Eve, the log is placed in the unlit fireplace. While members of the family sing traditional songs, each takes a turn bashing the log with a stick, coaxing it to "poop out" the candy and presents stuffed inside. (I wonder if that's where the expression "beat the crap out of" came from.)

Fun Facts: In Norway, people hide all their brooms on Christmas Eve to keep witches and evil spirits from getting their hands on them. In Italy, Santa Claus is actually an ugly, but kindly old witch named *La Befana*. Much like Santa, *La Befana* delivers toys to children. But don't leave out cookies and milk. *La Befana* prefers a plate of sausage, broccoli, and a glass of wine. (She *is* Italian, after all!)

Don't Look Now, But There's a Magnetron Behind You

Magnetron. It sounds like a villain from a sci-fi movie, doesn't it? But I bet you've got one in your house right now and you don't even know it.

If you do, you can thank the brilliant, self-taught Percy LeBaron Spencer for it. What's a magnetron? Read on and find out:

Spencer was born in 1894 in Howland, Maine. He didn't have an easy start. His father died when he was just 18 months old. His mother left him in the care of an aunt and uncle. When he was seven, his uncle died. (Geez!) With no one to support them, Spencer dropped out of grammar school and went to work at age 12 at a spool mill.

As a young teen, Spencer heard that a local paper mill would soon be adopting electricity, something barely heard of in his rural area. He set about learning as much as he could about it. Then he applied for work at the mill. Amazingly, he was one of only three people hired to install electricity in the plant, despite having no formal education or training in electrical engineering!

At 18, Spencer joined the US Navy as a radio operator. He'd developed a keen interest in wireless communications after reading about wireless operators when the Titanic sank. During long shifts at work, he set about making himself an expert on radio technology.

"I just got hold of a lot of textbooks and taught myself while I was standing watch at night," he explained. While he was at it, Spencer also taught himself trigonometry, calculus, chemistry, physics, and metallurgy. By 1939, Spencer was one of the world's leading experts in radar-tube design.

After being honorably discharged from the Navy after WWI, Spencer went to work for Raytheon as the chief of the power tube division. There he developed a more efficient way to manufacture magnetrons. (Finally, we get to the magnetrons!)

Magnetrons are high-powered vacuum tubes that generate short radio waves. When WWII broke out, they were used in radar systems to detect enemy planes and submarines. Spencer's work on these and other projects proved so vital to the war effort that he was awarded the Distinguished Public Service Award by the US Navy.

After WWII was over, one day Spencer was in a lab at Raytheon and noticed something peculiar. As he approached a magnetron, the chocolate bar in his pocket started melting. Intrigued, he decided to experiment with un-popped popcorn kernels. He held a bag of them up to the magnetron, and was surprised to hear the kernels start popping!

In yet another experiment, he put a raw egg in a tea kettle and held the magnetron over it. The egg exploded in his colleague's face! But there was no egg on Spencer's face. There was a big smile, instead. Because those short radio waves produced by the magnetron are actually *microwaves*. Percy Spencer had just discovered what would eventually become the *microwave oven*!

It would take about 20 years before his invention looked and performed like the ones we know today. The first commercial microwave, the "Radar-range" came out in 1947. It weighed about 750 pounds, stood six feet tall, and cost $5,000! (Equivalent to over $60,000 in 2021 dollars.)

Over his career with Raytheon, Spencer obtained over 300 patents. He died in 1970, and was posthumously inducted into the Inventors Hall of Fame in 1999.

Fun Facts: In 1967, the first reasonably-sized countertop microwave oven went on sale. It was produced by Amana (a division of Raytheon) and cost $495—or about $4,000 in today's dollars.

In 1945, Raytheon filed a US patent for the microwave cooking oven. For his invention, Spencer received no royalties. Instead, Raytheon paid him the same token payment it made to all inventors on its payroll at the time for company patents—a one-time gratuity of two dollars.

First Time for Everything

Given today's reality shows and cable channels, it seems that anything goes on TV nowadays. But it wasn't like that when the first television broadcast hit the airwaves in 1926.

On-air censorship kept things pretty straight-laced right up through the 1950s. Some words considered too vulgar to say on the air back then are almost laughable today, such as "water closet," and the term "pregnant."

As TV's popularity grew, many shows began testing the boundaries of what censors would allow. Here are some "TV firsts" we wouldn't even think twice about today:

Being Pregnant. Obviously pregnant women were a no-no in early TV. But in 1952, Lucille Ball was pregnant during an entire season of her hit show, *I Love Lucy*. To deal with it, the dreaded "P-word" wasn't allowed on the air. Instead, they referred to Lucy as "expecting," "with child," or "having a baby."

(Interesting side note: When Lucy and Ricky's first child was born in January 1953, nearly 72% of homes with TV sets tuned in to get a glimpse of the baby—substantially more than watched President Eisenhower be inaugurated the next day.)

Sexy Dance Moves. In 1956, Elvis made his first appearance on *The Ed Sullivan Show*. Sixty million viewers tuned in to watch (about 80% of viewers). After Elvis performed Little Richard's song, *Ready Teddy*, the cameras switched away from his gyrating hips and stayed on Elvis's upper torso so as not to over-stimulate the American public. By the third time Elvis appeared on the show, he was only shown from the waist up.

Toilets. In 1957, CBS yanked the pilot episode of *Leave It to Beaver* because of the plot. In it, two boys, Wally and Beaver, get a baby alligator by mail and hide it in toilet tank. But back then, showing a toilet on TV was a no-no! Only after all shots showing the toilet seat were edited out did censors give the episode the green light—making it the first time any part of a toilet (the tank) was shown on TV.

(Interesting side note: It would take until 1971 for a toilet flush to be heard (but not seen) on TV. Archie Bunker did the deed in an episode of *All in the Family*.)

Belly Buttons. From 1964-1966, navels were off limits on TV. Censors barred the bare belly button aspirations of Mary Ann on *Gilligan's Island*, Gidget on *Gidget*, and Jeannie on *I Dream of Jeannie*. It was Cher who finally broke the barrier in 1975, on the *Sonny & Cher Show*.

Interracial Kisses. In 1968, Captain Kirk and Lt. Uhura locked lips on *Star Trek*. While Kirk's character was always up to romantic shenanigans, this one made history as the first kiss aired involving characters of two different races. At the time, it was so controversial that some TV markets in the South refused to air the episode.

Cursing. It was almost time for the new millennium to begin when, in 1999, Mark Harmon uttered the first curse word on TV. It was a line given to his character on *Chicago Hope*. The groundbreaking phrase was, "S*%t happens." Well, it does *now* ...

Fun Fact: It was bound to happen—the first television commercial. (Ugh!) July 1, 1941, was the first day commercial advertising was officially allowed on television. Who ran the first ad? Bulova did, for their watches. The ad aired during a game between the Philadelphia Phillies and the Brooklyn Dodgers. It cost the company somewhere between $4 and $9 to run the static ad touting the name, Bulova.

There's Gold in Them There Balls

When it comes to trying to strike it rich, people have come up with all sorts of schemes and gimmicks. (Remember the pet rock?) But sometimes, there's money to be had right under your nose—or in this case, right under the water.

If you happen to live near a golf course, you might consider cashing in as a golf ball diver. As the name implies, this job entails retrieving golf balls from water hazards on and around golf courses. Once plucked from the depths, the balls, which cost the diver nothing, can be cleaned, repackaged, and resold to the courses and driving ranges from whence they came.

Sounds simple enough, right? But what does it pay? Golf ball divers typically work independently for various golf courses. The average salary for divers in the US is slightly over $52,000. Not bad, eh?

But the pay can be higher. *Much* higher, according to Florida resident and professional golf ball diver Glenn Berger.

Berger got into the game back when he was partly unemployed. Trying to earn a little money to make ends meet, he began sneaking onto a nearby golf course and stealing golf balls out of a lake. But his conscience got the better of him. Berger went legit with the golf course management, and soon his business took off like a tee-shot by Arnold Palmer.

Today, Berger travels around the state, scuba diving for lost golf balls. He estimates he collects between 1.3 and 1.7 million golf balls a year. After cleaning them in a chemical bath, he resells them to the golf courses and driving ranges for a buck a piece. Do the math, and Berger is raking in over a million dollars a year.

While it sounds like an easy way to make some dough, the job certainly isn't without its risks. First off, you have to be a pretty decent scuba diver. And, in Florida at least, it helps to be good at alligator wrestling, too.

Berger has had to deal with such encounters numerous times, risking life and limb as he shares the murky waters with the likes of gators, snakes, turtles, lawnmowers, tables, and even the occasional sunken golf cart. He says it's all par for the course in a regular work day.

Some say Berger's math is a little fishy. He'd have to collect close to 4,000 balls a day to add up to 1.5 million a year. Still, even at a tenth of that rate, the job sounds like a great way to score some pretty impressive greenbacks. Agreed?

Fun Facts: The modern-day game of golf was invented in Scotland in 1457 (predating Florida golf courses by quite a few centuries). More fun things about golf:

⬦ The first golf balls were made of feathers wrapped in leather.

⬦ The average golfer has a 12,500-to-1 chance of making a hole-in-one.

⬦ Golf was the first sport played on the moon. In 1971, astronaut Alan Shepard swung a makeshift 6-iron on the moon's surface—and missed the ball. (Inventing the moon mulligan!)

⬦ The longest successful putt on record was 110 feet, made by Jack Nicklaus during the 1964 Tournament of Champions.

A World Full of Weirdness

As far as I know, there's no law against being weird. This list of strange-but-true facts should help support my case:

- Canadians eat more macaroni and cheese than any other nation on the planet.
- A French general gave President John Quincy Adams a pet alligator. He kept it in a bathtub at the White House.
- On February 18, 1979, it snowed for 30 minutes in the Sahara desert.
- In Zimbabwe, it's illegal to make offensive gestures at a passing car.
- In 1825, Scotland tried to replicate the Parthenon. They never finished it. It's now nicknamed "Scotland's Disgrace."
- Back in the 1600s, tulips were a form of currency in Holland.
- In Milan, Italy, it's a legal requirement to smile at all times.
- In Switzerland it's illegal to own just one guinea pig because they are social animals and being kept alone is tantamount to abuse.
- In Israel, it's illegal to bring bears to the beach.
- The Bahamas has an uninhabited island known as Pig Beach. It's populated entirely by swimming pigs.
- It's illegal to flush the toilet after 10 p.m. in Switzerland.
- There's a town in India named Santa Claus.
- In New York, there's a tiny island called Just Room Enough, where there's just enough room for a tree and a house.
- In South Korea, only women give gifts on Valentine's Day, not men.
- Berlin, Germany instigated a new sport in 2008 called, "aggressive sitting." They sell special stools for it.
- In Greece, women are banned from wearing high heels or tall hats in the Olympic Stadium.
- In North Korea, citizens are legally allowed to have only one of 28 sanctioned haircut styles. Fourteen for men, fourteen for women.

Fun Facts: Let's face it. We humans are an odd lot. Here are some random acts of weirdness attributable only to good old *homo sapiens*:

- We can't taste anything without saliva.
- Dim lights reduce our appetites.
- We can't sneeze with our eyes open.
- Our eyes move about 50 times per second.
- We can't walk in a straight line without a visual point. Blindfolded, we gradually end up walking in a circle.

Business Secrets You Won't Read About in Forbes

If you're looking for stock tips, you won't find them here. Instead, you'll discover more weird and random things—this time about the monkey business that goes on behind the doors of government offices and big corporations.

Read on and find out just what I'm talking about:

The Star of the CIA. Deep inside the headquarters of the CIA is a place where nobody knows your name, and they prefer it that way. It's a Starbucks coffee shop. Due to matters of privacy and security, the CIA has its own Starbucks inside, where the baristas *never* write names on cups.

Friendly Walmart Spies. Those chummy greeters you run into at Walmart were originally put there to deter shoplifters.

Snooze, but don't Lose. In Japan, napping on the job is seen as a sign of diligence—as if you've worked yourself to the point of exhaustion. They call it *inemuri*, or basically, "present while sleeping."

Historic Car Theft. While Henry Ford made cars better, faster, cheaper, and more available to the general public, he didn't invent them, as many believe. That credit goes to Karl Benz. In 1885, Benz designed and created the first automobile powered by an internal combustion engine—a full year before Ford did.

Classic on the Cheap. In 1971, Nike paid graphic design student Carolyn Davidson just $35 for its now iconic "swoosh" logo. (As the company grew, she was awarded with 500 shares of Nike, as well as steady work.)

Secret Vault of Pain. If you've ever stepped on a LEGO, you know it can really hurt. But did you know LEGO has an underground vault that holds a collection of every single set they've ever made? Now you do!

Fake It Till You Make It. In 1961, a fledgling ice cream company sought a name that would evoke "old-world craftsmanship." Drawing on Danish heritage, they came up with Häagen-Dazs. What does it mean? Nothing. In the end, they just made it up.

Keeping Up Appearances. McDonald's golden arches are both iconic and regulation issue for franchises around the world. But there is one exception. After government officials declared the yellow to be too contrasting with the natural beauty of the red rock landscape, the McDonald's in Sedona, Arizona changed them to the color turquoise.

Fun Fact: The longest TV ad in history is 14 hours long. It was created by Old Spice fragrance, with supposedly "lasts forever." It aired in Brazil on December 8, 2018, earning it the Guinness World Record for the longest TV ad ever.

A Detective on a Dare

Back in the day, you might've found the author in this story munching on apples in the bathtub as she conjured up plots for her detective novels. During her career, she penned over 60 of them. And, as of last Tuesday, her books have sold more than two billion copies.

Who is she? Read on and find out!

Against her mother's wishes, Clarissa Miller taught herself to read. Spending most of her time alone with her imaginary friends, she had no formal education. But Miller *did* possess an extraordinary mind—one she put to good use entertaining her mother with stories plucked from her own imagination.

When Miller became sick with influenza, her mother suggested she start writing down her stories. And so was born her lifelong passion for writing.

Though Miller said she had no ambition to be a writer, when she was 11, a poem of hers was printed in a local London newspaper. By her late teens, several poems of hers had been published in *The Poetry Review*. But it was a challenge from her sister that caused her to write her first detective story.

It was about that time that Miller was sent to a finishing school in Paris. There, she was immersed in a world of military gentlemen, spinsters, widows, doctors, lords, and ladies. She used them in her stories, observing their rivalries, jealousies, and politics. (Miller herself was described as a "person who listened more than she talked, who saw more than she was seen.")

Miller jotted down her observations and notes in dozens of notebooks, saying "I usually have about half a dozen on hand ... to make notes in them of ideas that struck me, or about some poison or drug, or a clever little bit of swindling that I had read about in the paper."

In her autobiography, she's quoted as saying:

"Plots come to me at such odd moments, when I am walking along the street, or examining a hat shop...suddenly a splendid idea comes into my head."

Despite her enthusiasm and dedication to her craft, Miller wasn't an instant hit. After six consecutive rejections, it wasn't until 1920 that her first novel was finally published. Titled, *The Mysterious Affair at Styles*, it featured detective Hercule Poirot as the main character.

Do you know who it is now? Clarissa Miller is actually Agatha Clarissa Miller. When she married Archibald Christie in 1914, she became Agatha Christie.

A hundred years after her first book released, Agatha Christie's grandson, Mathew Prichard, explained her writing process.

"I think a book used to take her, in the 1950s, just a couple of months to write and then a month to revise before it was sent off to the publishers. She used to read the stories to us after dinner, one or two chapters at a time. I think we were ... her guinea pigs at that stage. Only my mother always knew who the murderer was. The rest of us were sometimes successful and sometimes not. My grandfather was usually asleep for most of the time."

I guess there's no escaping the critics, no matter who you turn out to be ...

Fun Fact: The first detective story in print is credited to Edgar Allan Poe. His short story, *The Murders in the Rue Morgue*, appeared in *Graham's Lady's and Gentleman's Magazine* in 1841. In it, Poe describes the extraordinary "analytical power" possessed by Monsieur C. Auguste Dupin in solving the brutal murders of two women in Paris.

The Cure is Worse than the Disease

Today, it seems like we've got a pill to cure everything from toenail fungus to cancer. What you might not know is, way back when, there was a cure for everything, too. But you just might not survive it.

Here's a look at a few "cures" that may have been worse than the diseases they were meant to treat:

Wretched Rabies Cure. Back in Roman times, people thought they could cure rabies by cutting open the wound and covering it with raw veal. After that, the patient was to eat a diet of lime and hog fat. If they survived *that* phase, the third would surely do them in. It involved drinking a concoction made of wine and boiled badger dung. Uh, I think I'd rather just die ...

Magical Malaria Cure. Those Romans were an interesting bunch. One physician in the 3rd Century instructed malaria sufferers to write the word, "abracadabra" over and over on a piece of paper, with one less letter on each line, until the letters formed a triangle with a single letter "a" at the bottom.

Once done, the paper was to be tied around the neck with flax and worn for nine days before tossing the paper into an east-running stream. If that didn't work? Victims could try rubbing themselves down with lion fat. Hmm. I wonder if they sell that at Food Lion ...

The Cystic Hand of Fate. Anyone unfortunate enough to come down with cysts on their hands or wrists could find a cure with the German anatomist Lorenz Heister. In 1743, he wrote that cysts could be treated by strapping a bullet to them that had killed an animal. An alternate cure was to touching the cysts with a dead man's hand. Those failing, one could hit the cysts with a heavy book—preferably the Bible. All-righty then ...

Spice Up Your Mood. A Welsh manuscript from 1382 entitled, *The Red Book of Hergest*, contains many herbal remedies. One of them was a sure-fire way to "remove drunkenness."

Besotted patients were advised to "eat bruised saffron with spring water." Saffron also cured sadness, according to the book. It advised, "If you would be at all times merry, eat saffron in meat or drink, and you will never be sad: but beware of eating over-much, lest you should die of excessive joy." (Given today's rate of $60 an ounce for saffron, there's not much chance of overindulging, is there?)

A Whole Body of Cures. Suffering from headaches? Epilepsy? Bruises? In the 16th and 17th centuries, dead human bodies became popular cures for nearly anything that ailed a person. Corpses were in such demand that Egyptian tombs and graveyards were looted for them. Powder made from bodies was to be applied to the skin, or ingested via a drink. It may sound crazy today, but everyone did it back then—including Francis Bacon and French King Francis I.

Fun Fact: Back in the 1740s, a British evangelist named John Wesley published the *Primitive Physick, An Easy and Natural Method of Curing Most Diseases.* Some remedies included were:

- Soothe heart palpitations by drinking "a pint of cold water," then "apply outwardly a rag dipt in vinegar," and "be electrified."
- Treat asthma with "a fortnight on boiled carrots only."
- Prevent nosebleeds by holding "a red-hot poker under the nose or steep a linen rag in sharp vinegar, burn it, and blow it up the nose with a quill." (Yikes!)

Spying in Plain Sight

You have to admit, James Bond is cool. I mean, who doesn't secretly wish they were 007? It may surprise you to learn this, but the guy who created the most famous and successful secret agent of all time actually was one himself!

Before Ian Fleming created James Bond, he was an intelligence officer for the British Navy. During WWII, he served as Lieutenant Commander with the Naval Intelligence Division. As such, Fleming conducted numerous Bond-like operations himself, including the Navy's Operation Golden Eye.

Golden Eye was a top-secret plan to provide defense support for Gibraltar in case Germany invaded through Spain. The attack never happened, so the plan wasn't put into action. But that didn't stop Fleming from using the name.

GoldenEye was the title of the 17th book in the Bond series. (*GoldenEye* was also the first film in which Pierce Brosnan played the starring role as 007.)

In addition, GoldenEye was the name Fleming gave his home in Jamaica. It was here in 1952 where Fleming began writing his first Bond spy novel, *Casino Royale*. He finished it in two months, using inspiration drawn from both his experiences and his imagination.

(For those unfamiliar, *Casino Royale*, as would all the subsequent Bond novels, centers around the exploits of an officer in the UK Secret Intelligence Service, commonly known as MI6. Agent James Bond is given the code number 007.)

But Fleming wasn't exactly thrilled with his writing in *Casino Royale*. Upon its completion, he called his work a "dreadful, oafish opus." At first, most readers of the unpublished draft seemed to agree.

Fleming's friend, William Plomer, remarked of it, "So far as I can see the element of suspense is completely absent." Even so, the manuscript was forwarded it to the publishing house Jonathan Cape. They were less than enthusiastic as well. But because they managed Fleming's brother Peter's books, they were persuaded to give it a try.

Good thing, too. On April 13, 1953, *Casino Royale* was released in hardcover in the UK, bearing a cover designed by Fleming himself. It was a smash success. Three print runs were needed to keep up with demand!

In an in interview with *The New Yorker* in 1962, Fleming explained, "When I wrote the first one in 1953, I wanted Bond to be an extremely dull, uninteresting man to whom things happened; I wanted him to be a blunt instrument."

Well, as Bond fans know, *that* was one mission that most assuredly did *not* get accomplished. In fact, with each book, the Bond series got even more popular. The films even more so. The last Bond film, *No Time to Die*, released October 8, 2021. It grossed over $55 million on opening weekend alone!

Fun Fact: How did Fleming arrive at the name of his hero, James Bond? In a way, it was a birdbrain idea. You see, Fleming was a keen birdwatcher. One day he looked at a bird guide, *Birds of the West Indies*, and noticed the name of the American ornithologist who had authored the book—James Bond.

Fleming told his wife, "this brief, unromantic, Anglo-Saxon and yet very masculine name was just what I needed." Later, he explained in his interview with *The New Yorker*, "When I was casting around for a name for my protagonist, I thought by God, it's the dullest name I ever heard."

Maybe You Should Quit Your Day Job ...

Lots of famous historical figures had another profession altogether before fate intervened to rocket them to fame (and sometimes fortune). Check out these surprising day jobs these people had before they left them behind to pursue loftier goals:

Thomas Jefferson. A true Renaissance man, Jefferson's interests not only spanned politics, but also linguistics, music, science, and architecture. But he had yet another interest not widely known: archaeology.

Jefferson employed his knowledge of Native American languages to better understand their cultures. And when he found a tribal burial mound near his home in Virginia, he decided to dig it up. His act was the first scientific archaeological site in the US. Carefully noting his findings, in 1787 Jefferson included a written entry in his book, *Notes on the State of Virginia*, creating America's first published paper on archaeology.

Paul Revere. Most remembered for his legendary Midnight Ride to warn colonists during the American Revolution, a closer look at Revere reveals there's much more history to sink your teeth into. He also became a silversmith working beside his father in the family business, but hard times forced Revere to expand his horizons to dentistry.

After the bloody Battle of Bunker Hill, the family of a noted general killed during the fight wanted to give their kin a proper burial. But the general had been placed in a mass grave with other soldiers. Decomposition made it impossible to identify him.

Revere stepped in to help. He noticed one of the bodies had a dental prosthetic just like one he'd made for his client, the general. His body was identified, and Revere made history yet again. This time, as instigating the first time in US history whereby a member of the military was identified through forensic dentistry.

Nostradamus. Internationally famous for his cryptic quatrains predicting the future, few people know that the legendary seer also wrote cookbooks. One of his most notable was the *Treatise on Make-up and Jam*. In it, Nostradamus included his own recipe for "love jam," a concoction so powerful it would drive couples to engage in the act of love if they tasted it together. Other recipes in the book included cures for the plague and constipation, and a way to turn one's hair blonde. Huh. Maybe the guy really *could* foresee the future.

Fun Fact: As of August 22, 2022, the best-selling cookbook of all time was *Joy of Cooking* by Irma S. Rombauer. Published in 1931, it's full of tried-and-true favorites. To date, it has sold over 20 million copies and has garnered nearly 200,000 ratings on Goodreads.

T-Rex Chickens Out

Until fairly recently, dinosaurs were thought to be cold-blooded, slow-moving reptiles with scaly skin and dim brains. It wasn't until the 1970s that this popular theory began to be seriously challenged. In 1986, a book by paleontologist Robert Bakker, summed up the evidence that dinosaurs were warm-blooded, agile creatures that had more in common with birds than lizards.

Though highly controversial at the time, Bakker's book, *The Dinosaur Heresies*, has come to represent much of today's current prevailing beliefs—at least in paleontological circles. One of the biggest hurdles in the scientific debate was whether dinosaurs were cold- or warm-blooded. Bakker's book argued the point with such facts as:

- Some dinosaurs lived in northern latitudes where cold-blooded creatures couldn't survive.
- To pump blood up long-necked dinosaurs like the Brontosaurus would require the four-chambered heart of a warm-blooded animal.
- Dinosaurs grew rapidly, unlike cold-blooded animals.
- Almost every animal that walks upright today is warm-blooded, and dinosaurs walked upright.

The debate raged on for decades. The case to prove dinosaurs were warm-blooded was still circumstantial—until a quirk of fate changed all that.

In 2003, scientists Jack Horner and Mary Schweitzer discovered some *T. rex* bones in a remote section of Montana. They wanted to fly the bones out, but the femur was too large to fit inside their helicopter.

So they broke it in half.

To their amazement, inside the bone was some material that hadn't fossilized. While they couldn't recover DNA from the *T. rex*, they did retrieve molecules of collagen.

Collagen's structure varies slightly in different animals. The scientists compared the dinosaur's version with the collagen of 21 living animals, including humans, chimps, mice, alligators, chickens, salmon, and ostriches.

The result? The closest match was to chickens and ostriches. The second closest match was to alligators. Obviously, this didn't exactly clear the muddy waters. Much more research is definitely needed before we know who *T. Rex* owes all that back child support to.

But for now, it would appear that his closest living relative is the chicken. Like their huge, short-armed father, chickens are warm-blooded, have three-toed feet, and look funny when they run. In addition, *T. rex* swallowed stones to help churn and grind up food, much like chickens use their gizzards today.

Interesting, huh? If Bakker turns out to be right, it could be that the gizzard killed the lizard—at least in theory, anyway.

Fun Fact: The seven *Jurassic Park* movies helped popularize the idea that dinosaurs are quick, smart, and birdlike. The first film, *Jurassic Park*, premiered in June of 1993. It instantly became the highest-grossing film released worldwide up to that date, earning $50.1 million in its first weekend.

How Harry Met Henry

With a name like Margaret, I fall subject to all kinds of nicknames—often casually flung at me by people who can scarcely believe I would want to use my full given name. (Margaret? The horrors!) Instead, they call me Maggie, Margie, Peggy, Mag, Meggy, or even Martha. (I guess those are still better than the old-time nicknames, Mog and Daisy.)

But some nicknames seem totally off the mark. For instance, how in the world did William become Bill? Read on and find out:

How Edward became Ted. Back in the Middle Ages, there weren't that many first names to choose from. What was a poor peasant to do to differentiate between people? I know! Swap letters around. Huh?

For names that began with a vowel, it was common to replace the first letter with a consonant. So why didn't Edward become "Ded"? Well, for obvious reasons. Plus, due to illiteracy and lack of dentistry, "T" was often easier to pronounce than "D." So Edward became Ted, a nickname also shared by Theodore.

How Richard became Dick. Back in the 12th and 13th centuries (way before computers and Kinkos copy shops), everything had to be written by hand. Long names like Richard were a chore. So to save time, weary scribes shortened them to Rich or Rick.

Rhyming nicknames were also popular. Rich turned into Hitch, and Rick into Hick and Dick. Given the choice between being a Hick or a Dick, the latter choice won out. In fact, Dick became so popular it was picked to be in "Every Tom, Dick, or Harry," a phrase used to describe the swelling throngs of "Everyman."

How Charles became Chuck. In Middle English, the name Charles was Chukken. This is probably the origin of the nickname. But back then, the phrase, "Dear Chuck," was a term of endearment, just like "Darling."

Shakespeare even used the phrase in his play, *Macbeth*, when referring to Lady Macbeth. I wonder, would a Charles by any other name still be a Chuck?

How William became Bill. Well, to explain this oddity, we have to go back again to the Middle Ages' trend of letter swapping and rhyming. Because hard consonants were easier to pronounce, many believe Will morphed into Bill for phonetic reasons. Adding credence to this theory, during the 17th century reign of William III over England, subjects mockingly called him "King Billy."

How Henry became Hank. The name Henry goes way back to medieval England. One theory on how Hank entered the picture was that Hendrick is the Dutch form of the name Henry. Henk was the nickname for Hendrick, and thus morphed into Hank.

How John became Jack. Well, we can't blame this one on achy-handed scribes, letter-swapping, or easier-to-pronounce consonants. So, what gives? The timeless art of sarcasm, perhaps. You see, the name Jack used to be a generic term for a peasant. Peasants with a trade eventually became lumberjacks, steeplejacks, etc. Even the term jackass finds its roots here.

Meanwhile, John was also once a generic name for peasants and commoners (John Doe). So Jack became a fitting nickname for John. Or, at least, that's one theory. Another is that the Normans added "kin" to the end of a noun when they wanted to make a nickname. So John became Jenkin, and, over time, turned into Jakin, which ultimately became Jack.

How Henry became Harry. Henry was a popular name among British monarchs. Following a long-standing tradition, many of them preferred to be called Harry by their subjects. The tradition continues to this day, with Prince Henry of Wales going by Prince Harry. Today, Harry is not just a nickname, but a popular given name, perhaps fueled by the popularity of the fictional character, Harry Potter.

Fun Fact: While James, Robert, and John have been the most popular boy's names of the past 100 years, they are getting a run for their money. In 2022, the most popular boy's names in the US were, in ranking order: Liam, Noah, Oliver, and Elijah.

Mugging for the Camera

It takes a special kind of talent to make it in showbiz. Fred Muggs had something no other person in Hollywood could claim before *or* since. What exactly was his claim to fame? Read on and find out:

Muggs was born March 14, 1952, and arrived in New York City before his first birthday. While still a youngster, his unique looks and talents were spotted by a pair of former pages for NBC, and soon Muggs was offered a spot on the *Perry Como Show*.

Pat Weaver of the *Today Show* saw Muggs' potential and set up an audition for him there. The *Today Show* had just gotten on the air, and the ratings were bad. But when Muggs joined the cast as co-host with host Dave Garroway, ratings began to climb. Soon, advertisers began vying for the right to run commercials during the show.

Jim Fleming, the original newsreader for the show, didn't like Muggs, so he quit. Muggs took over "reading" the day's newspapers, as well as imitating Popeye and playing the piano with Steve Allen.

Big deal. What's so amazing about that? Well, you see, Fred Muggs was a chimpanzee.

After being named Mr. Muggs in a contest, the *Today Show* added the J. Fred to his moniker. During his career on the *Today Show*, Muggs learned more than 500 words and had a wardrobe of 450 different outfits. As his fame grew, books, comics, and games featured his likeness. Muggs was even called upon to open supermarkets and commission US Navy ships!

The *Today Show*'s producer, Richard Pinkham, once estimated Muggs had brought the network $100 million in revenues.

In addition to acting, Muggs was also an artist. One of his finger paintings was used as the cover of *Mad* magazine in 1958. The magazine even ran an article spoofing the show, warning of "J. Floyd Gluggs'" ambition to take over the anchor spot.

Muggs went on a world tour to promote the *Today Show*. In Japan, his popularity was second only to Marilyn Monroe! While in Russia, a paper there described Muggs as "a symbol of the American way of life," and said he was "necessary in order that the average American should not look into reports on rising taxes and decreasing pay, but rather laugh at the funny mug of a chimpanzee."

In 1957, Muggs was replaced by another chimp called Kokomo Jr. In a press release, NBC stated Muggs intended "to extend his personal horizons."

Fun Facts: After leaving the *Today Show*, Muggs briefly starred in *The J. Fred Muggs Show* before heading to Tampa, Florida to work at Busch Gardens. Before retiring to Citrus Park, Florida with his "live-in girlfriend" Phoebe B. Beebie, Muggs celebrated his 23rd birthday with an appearance on *Good Morning America* on ABC. As of 2022, Muggs was still alive and enjoying retirement.

What a Way to Go!

Some people want to be cremated and have their ashes spread in the ocean or a field of wildflowers. Others want a traditional funeral, along with a service and flowers. Still others opt for something entirely different.

Check out these celebrities who went out with a bang ...

Jimmy Dean. This country music legend didn't leave anything to chance when it came to his last respects. The inventor of the pancake-wrapped breakfast corndog left instructions for his own lavish entombment—inside a $350,000 piano-shaped mausoleum. His final request? That the piano be inscribed with the words. "Here lies one hell of a man." His final wish was granted.

James Doohan. Best known as engineer "Scotty" on *Star Trek*, it was only fitting he requested to be buried in space. Doohan's ashes were launched into orbit on a rocket operated by a private company.

Tupac Shakur. The famous rapper actually never had a funeral. The private ceremony planned by his mother was cancelled, and he was cremated. Shakur's crew, the Outlawz, mixed his ashes with weed and smoked him.

Jim Henson. The genius creator of the Muppets had two memorial services—one in London and one in New York. At these "Life celebrations," it was Henson's wish that no one wear black. During both ceremonies, Big Bird himself sang "It's Not Easy Being Green." Services ended with a team of Muppeteers singing Henson's favorite songs, and the Dixieland Jazz Band playing "When the Saints Go Marching In."

Evel Knievel. The motorcycle daredevil's funeral was held in a stadium that could seat 17,000. The service included a speech by Matthew McConaughey and a fireworks show. Knievel was buried in his leather jacket with patriotic red and blue trim.

James Brown. When the Godfather of Soul passed away in 2006, his funeral was quite the performance. Actually it was *three* performances, as the R&B legend had three different funerals! The first was held at Harlem's Apollo

Theatre. There, Brown's body was placed in a gold Promethean casket and drawn through the streets in a white, horse-drawn carriage.

Brown's second funeral took place at the James Brown Arena in Augusta, Georgia. Brown's bands and legends like Little Richard and Stevie Wonder entertained 8,000 mourners, who were also served food. No quiet affair, it was attended by all sorts of luminaries and dignitaries—including a surprise appearance by Michael Jackson, who called Brown his greatest inspiration.

A third private funeral was held in Brown's native South Carolina. It took nearly two and a half months for Brown to finally be interred at his daughter's home in Beech Island. While family disagreements were settled, Brown's body lay in its casket in cold storage at a funeral home.

Fun Fact: In the 1980s, Fredric Baur, the founder of Pringles potato chips, requested to be buried in a Pringles can. His children honored his request.

Abracadabra, I'm Back!

A bird that can't fly is kind of like a fish that can't swim. I mean, what's the point? There must be one Mother Nature isn't sharing with us, because, believe it or not, going flightless isn't exactly a rare occurrence in the bird family.

In the past, there used to be hundreds of species of flightless birds, including owls, ibis, woodpeckers, finches, and hoopoes. With no predators around, they didn't need wings. Unfortunately, when humans began colonizing every region of the world, *we* became the predators. In a few hundred years, we hunted over 150 flightless species to extinction.

Today, around 60 species of flightless birds still roam our planet. Most are penguins, ostriches, rails, and their relatives. The rest are extinct forever ... or are they?

A recent finding is proving there may be hope for our fine, flightless friends to reappear, sort of like magic. The process of returning from extinction is called *reiterative evolution*. The perfect example of it is the Aldabra rail.

Around 136,000 years ago, the atoll in the Indian Ocean where the flightless rails lived was inundated by a major flood, wiping them out along with all the other animals who couldn't fly or swim to safety.

Over tens of thousands of years, sea levels receded until the atoll was again above water. At some point, white-throated rails flew there and colonized the island. With no predators on the atoll, flying again became unnecessary. In less than 20,000 years, the white-throated rail had tapped into its ancient gene pool and re-morphed into the flightless subspecies called the Aldabra rail.

The Aldabra rail proves that when conditions are right, species can re-emerge over and over, despite past generations going extinct. Iterative evolution could just be Mother Nature's magic secret. I wonder if I can get her to use it to bring back the Klondike Choco Taco ...

Fun Fact: The dodo bird is perhaps the most well-known example of a flightless bird made extinct by man. How did that come to be?

Dutch sailors first recorded mention of the dodo in 1598. Native to the island of Mauritius, a fully grown dodo stood over three feet tall and weighed up to 39 pounds. (That's surprising, considering its closest living relative is a pigeon.) The last sighting of a live dodo was in 1662. Today, the only remnants of the species are drawings, skeletons, and a single dried head.

The dodo's extinction in less than a century called attention to man's impact on the environment. The bird's role in the story of *Alice's Adventures in Wonderland* helped popularize the dodo and immortalized it as a symbol of both extinction and obsolescence. The lesson here? Don't be a dodo.

A Vacation Like No Other

Looking for something different to do with your time off this year? Have a penchant for odd things? (Of course you do. You're reading this book, aren't you?)

Here are some vacation destinations you've probably never heard about, but definitely top the list for oddest ways to spend a day in the US of A.

The Ben and Jerry's Flavor Graveyard. Still mourning the fact your favorite flavor was killed off? Head to the Waterbury Village Historic District in Vermont and pay your respects at one of the coolest graveyards in the world.

Honoring "The Dearly De-Pinted," the place looks like a tiny cemetery. But a closer look at the headstones reveal the final resting places for discontinued flavors such as Aloha Macadamia, Fossil Fuel, etc.

The Great Gum Wall of Seattle. Admit it. You've done it before—stuck your chewed gum up under a desk or table. Well, in Seattle, the habit has risen to a gooey art form.

In the 1990s, someone waiting in line for a show stuck their gum on the wall of the alley by Market Theater. For some reason known only to gum chewers, the alley soon became ground zero for worn-out gum. Recently, 2,350 pounds of gum was pried from the walls. Days later, it began to sprout again. I suppose that's one way to leave your mark on the world, isn't it?

The Museum of Bad Art (MOBA). Founded in 1994, this privately-owned museum in Boston is dedicated to celebrating "the labor of artists whose work would be displayed and appreciated in no other forum." Its permanent collection includes over 700 pieces of art "too bad to be ignored."

To be included in MOBA, works must be original and have serious intent, but also contain significant flaws. No kitsch or boring stuff allowed. Think you've painted the next "disasterpiece"? Bring it along and find out!

The Glass Beach. What road trip is complete without a trip to the ocean? Head to Fort Bragg, California and check out a shoreline covered in glass garbage.

From 1906 to 1967, the place was a dumping ground, with people literally throwing their garbage over the cliffs there. Eventually, the glass refuse began showing up as pieces polished smooth by sand and waves. The beach is protected, so you can't take any finds with you, but you can take all the pictures you want.

Protected garbage. Is that really something to Bragg about?

The National Mustard Museum. Crazy about condiments? Then you just might get your fill at this one-of-a-kind exhibit in Middleton, Wisconsin. The museum was opened in 1992 by Barry Levenson, who had amassed an astounding collection of mustard and mustard-related memorabilia. At the museum, you can learn how mustard is made, view over 5,500 types of mustard on display, and even belly up to the mustard bar and sample hundreds of flavors on tap.

The Corn Palace. Why bother with that long trip to the Taj Mahal when the US has its own palace in Mitchell, South Dakota? This is no corny joke. Over half a million visitors plow their way to it each year.

Built in 1892 as a testament to agriculture, The Corn Palace features intricate, mosaic-like designs on both the interior and exterior of the massive, ornamental structure. Highlights include pillars that look like corn, and themed murals made of corn that are updated and changed each year.

Leila's Hair Museum. Have you ever wondered what hairdressers do with all the hair they trim from clients? (Me either.) Anyway, if your hairdresser is Leila Cohoon, chances are good your hair is now enjoying a second life as art in her museum.

Located in Independence, Missouri, Leila's Hair Museum boasts more than 400 wreaths made from braided hair and over 2,000 pieces of jewelry hand-crafted from human hair. She even has a few locks of hair from President Lincoln and Marilyn Monroe. If you ask me, that's a big, hairy deal.

Carhenge. Who cares about a bunch of old rocks called Stonehenge, when you can see the same thing made out of cars near Alliance, Nebraska? Fashioned after the ancient stone monoliths in England, Carhenge was built in 1987 using old cars painted gray to make them look more like stones. You might be asking, uh...why? The answer, according to Carhenge creator Jim Reinders, is, "Why not?" Why not, indeed.

Fun Fact: The worst part about road trips is finding a bathroom, am I right? Visit these odd attractions and you won't have to hunt down a loo:

- The world's largest toilet is in Kids Commons hands-on museum in Columbus, Indiana. It's large enough for an adult to sit inside. (Not that you'd want to.)
- The world's most scenic urinal is at the Hotel Kona in Hawaii. Open to the public, it features a window wall looking out to breathtaking views of the ocean.

Bedtime for Bongo

Decades before Walt Disney set foot in the Sunshine State, another man set his sights on building a theme park in Florida. He was a dermatologist named Dr. Perry Sperber.

In the 1940s, Sperber leased several acres of land in the coastal town of Port Orange that was once home to a sugar mill plantation. The doctor then set about creating a most unusual amusement park amid the ruins. It was part tram ride, part gardens, part zoo, and part "what-the-heck?"

Once completed in 1948, Sperber's theme park boasted live animals, a replica of a Seminole Indian village, and a miniature-train tram-ride that took passengers past "prehistoric monsters" sculpted from concrete and chicken wire by a local cement worker named Manny Lawrence.

Sperber quite aptly named his creation, "Bongoland," after a baboon he'd procured as a park attraction.

From 1948 to 1952, visitors flocked—well, they meandered up to—Bongoland. Sadly it closed only four years after opening. A sign on the premises gave the reason as "lack of public interest."

But times and interests change. Bongoland now has a new name and a new lease on life. The 12 acres have been renamed Sugar Mill Gardens—and admission is free! Visitors can stroll among flowering trees, bushes, and native flora. Sharp-eyed ones might also spot a few of Bongoland's old monsters hiding out among the plants!

Amazingly, four of the concrete dinosaurs still survive, and lurk amongst the grounds as protected relics of Florida's heritage. Among them are a 25-foot-long Triceratops, and an impressive Stegosaurus. (There used to be a 42-foot-tall T-Rex, but it collapsed into rubble during a rainstorm in July 2019.)

Fancy a peek for yourself? Head to Port Orange and check it out! It's open daily from 8 a.m. to 5 p.m.

Fun Fact: Bongoland isn't the only dinosaur theme park to go extinct. Dinosaur World, a 65-acre park in Beaver, Arkansas featured 100 life-sized sculptures of dinosaurs, cavemen, and even King Kong before it closed.

Another bygone park is Bedrock City in Custer, South Dakota. It featured characters from the Flintstones cartoon show. It shut its doors in 2015, and reopened as a budget campground called Buffalo Ridge Camp Resort of the Black Hills.

Sorry you missed Fred and Wilma at Bedrock City? No worries! There's another park just like it that's still open in Valle, Arizona. You'll find it under the name Raptor Ranch.

All You Gotta Do is "Act Naturally"

Ever dreamed of the limelight? Or at least the hefty paycheck? It could happen when you least expect it! Here are stories of extraordinary celebrities who were discovered while doing very ordinary things.

Marilyn Monroe was 19 when she was discovered by a photographer while working in a munitions factory.

Eva Mendes wanted to be a nun, but Hollywood came knocking when a talent agent spotted a picture of her *at her neighbor's house!*

Vin Diesel was only seven years old when a director caught him and his friends breaking into a theater. Rather than busting them, she cast them in her upcoming production.

Justin Bieber got his big break when music manager Scooter Braun accidentally clicked on one of Bieber's YouTube videos while looking for someone else.

Tracy Chapman was attending Tufts University when her classmate stole one of her demos and sent it to his father, who was a music executive.

Pamela Anderson was at a BC Lions football game when the Jumbotron camera pointed her way. She was wearing a Labatt's Beer shirt. The brewing company hired her as their spokesmodel, turning her into an instant celebrity.

Danny Trejo, a recovering drug addict and former jailbird, was working as a youth drug counselor when one of his clients, a young actor, asked him to come with him to a film set to support him. Trejo got cast as an extra in a prison scene, and his career took off.

John Wayne, a former football player, was pushing props around a set when a producer was captivated by his wholesomeness and put him in his movie.

Will Smith had made—and lost—a fortune as a rap singer. A chance meeting with a talent developer in the parking lot of Universal Studios landed him his first role as the lead in *The Fresh Prince of Bel-Air*.

Chris Pratt was living in a van and waiting tables when a director came in to the restaurant where he worked. She said, "Hey, you're cute, do you act?" He said, "Yeah, I act. You should put me in a movie." Four days later, he was in LA. He never looked back.

Charlize Theron bought a one-way ticket from South Africa to LA when she was just 18. Almost broke and living in a sketchy hotel, she nearly lost it when a bank teller wouldn't cash her check. Hearing Theron yelling, a man came over and offered to help. He turned out to be a talent agent. Impressed by her "performance," he gave Theron her big break.

Fun Facts: The idea for the Hollywood Walk of Fame was conceived in 1953 by the volunteer president of the Hollywood Chamber of Commerce. In August 1958, the first eight stars were installed. Today, the Walk of Fame has over 2600 stars and spans 15 blocks of Hollywood Boulevard—about 1.3 miles, plus an extra three blocks on Vine Street. Installing a new star on the walk today costs $55,000.

A Ball to Build a Dream On

Wish you could pick the winning lottery numbers? You and me both, my friend!

Lots of people hope that Lady Luck will work her magic through a combination of special dates, such as anniversaries and family-members' birthdays. Others look for inspiration from above, and "signs," such as numbers that keep recurring on clocks, road signs and license plates.

Working out a system to pick winning numbers is nothing new. It's been around since before the lottery as we know it today was even around. How is that possible? Because before the lottery, there was *bolita*.

Bolita means "little ball" in Spanish. A popular game in the 1800s and early 1900s, bolita was a prelude to today's lottery. To play, people picked a number from 1-100, in hopes the ball with their number on it would be drawn from a sack full of 100 wooden or ivory balls. If their number came up, they won the jackpot.

The game originated in France after the French Revolution, but quickly spread to Spain, then Cuba, then to Key West, Florida. Before long, it became popular throughout the state, with bar owners using bolita as a way to get customers in the door.

With an 80-to-1 payoff, it was enticing for people to put down a nickel or dime and take their chances. But which number should they pick? To encourage players to risk their cash, a list was created that claimed to foretell winning numbers based on what images appeared in players' dreams. Here it is:

- Bad Boy—41 Bad Year—45 Barrel—70
- Bed—57 Beggar—83 Bird—91
- Black Dog—71 Black Crow—34
- Black Woman—73 Blood—48 Boat—56
- Bright Sun—60 Bull—16 Butterfly—2
- Cat—4 Chicken—38 Church—55 Clock—67

- Cow—44 Dead—8 Deer—32 Dog—15
- Duck—42 Drunk—52 Eel—27 Elephant—9
- Eyeglasses—88 Fine Cat—20 Fire—100
- Flags—77 Flowers—50 Freighter—79
- Frog—22 Full Moon—80 Funeral—98
- Goat—29 Hog—33 Home—1 Jail—65
- Knife—68 Lamb—43 Lamp—62
- Large Corpse—64 Large Fish—10 Lion—92
- Mirror—85 Mockingbird—97 Monkey—35
- Moon—17 Mule—54 Nun—5 Necktie—75
- Old House—89 Old Lady—82 Old Man—90
- Peacock—13 Pigeon—24 Pineapple—74
- Pipe—37 Police—51 Precious Stone—26
- Prostitute—12 Rabbit—40 Raccoon—47
- Rat—30 Razor—81 Revolver—61 Ring—59
- Roach—49 Rooster—11 Safe—76
- Sailboat—39 Sailor—3 Sarcophagi—78
- Saw—72 Sea—84 Seashell—7 & 25 Ship—23
- Shoes—96 Shrimp—31 Small Fish—18
- Snake—21 Spider—36 Squirrel—86 Star—66
- Street Car—46 Stone Crab—58 Storm—99
- Suckers—69 Swivel—95 Sword—63
- Tiger—14 Tragedy—53 Trunk—87
- Turtle—6 Vest Chain—94 War—93
- Wasp—28 Worm—19

As you can see, the list above reflects both the lifestyle at the time *and* the dangerous roots of bolita.

In the early days of bolita, law enforcement allowed it to go on because of the low wagers involved. But when prohibition ended and moonshine profits dried up, organized crime infiltrated the bolita circuit.

By the 1950s, millions of dollars were being bet on bolita. Local law enforcement vice squads turned up the heat, and soon the golden goose was cooked.

Fun Fact: You might have noticed one of the dream images is a swivel (95). What's a swivel? It's a gun mounting that secures a weapon, but allows it to swing around in any direction—such as on a tank or a boat. As to why numbers 7 and 25 are both seashells, only the bolita list-master knows for sure ...

A Man with a Lot of Baggage

Born in 1931, Hugo Doyle Owens was not a man of means, but he *was* a man with a plan. Even though his pockets were empty, his entrepreneurial spirit was unstoppable.

With a borrowed pickup truck and a $300 loan, he would go on to build a retail institution from what some would call a pile of discarded rubbish. By the time he passed away in 2016 at the age of 85, Owens had created a one-of-a-kind merchandise operation visited by over a million customers a year.

But before Owens could climb his unique ladder to success, he had to get rid of some major baggage—quite literally. In 1972, Owens was barely eking out a living selling insurance in Scottsboro, Alabama when a chance conversation with a friend would change the trajectory of his life.

Owen's friend worked for Trailways bus lines. When he told Owen about all the unclaimed luggage Trailways stored at its Washington, D.C. operations, something clicked inside Owens' mind. Borrowing a truck and $300, he drove to Trailways and bought all the bags he could afford.

"We looked like Jed Clampett's clan coming back down from Washington, D.C., to Alabama," Owens said in an interview with his grandson Benjamin.

Once he got back home, Owens and his wife, Mollie Sue, rented a house and set up tables in the front yard to display the goods they found inside the unclaimed baggage. They sold out the very first day.

Encouraged by their success, Owens bought up more unclaimed luggage from bus lines. Soon, he expanded his ambitious gambit to airlines, which had way more misplaced bags lying around. What lay inside them was anybody's guess.

"We never know what's in those suitcases until we open them," Owens said in 1978. "It's like buying a pig in a poke."

Some of the more memorable items he and his employees discovered inside the unclaimed bags they bought include:

- A live rattlesnake
- A 42-carat emerald
- A suit of armor
- Egyptian artifacts dating to 1500 BC

Before long, the business got so big that Owen opened up a storefront, calling it the Unclaimed Baggage center. After that, business took off like a jet engine.

"This is just American ingenuity," said Brett Snyder, president of *Cranky Flier*, an airline industry blog. "Finding a niche opportunity and putting it to use."

Today, employees decide which unclaimed items will be sold, donated, or discarded. Typical items on display at Unclaimed Baggage include shoes, electronics, jewelry, and, of course, clothing—which is dry-cleaned on site. Items sell for 20% to 80% off retail.

Owen retired in 1995, but his family still runs the business. Today, over a million people from across the US and other countries visit Unclaimed Baggage each year. To keep up with demand, the facility has expanded to a cavernous 40,000 square-foot store bigger than a city block. It's so huge, in fact, that there's an on-site café and store map to help you plan your treasure hunt.

Why not plan a visit yourself? Like Owen said, there's no telling what you might find inside.

Fun Fact: Chances are, if you lose your luggage, it will end up at Unclaimed Baggage in Scottsboro, Alabama. The business relationships Owen built over the years with bus lines and airlines are still strong, and every day, at least 5,000 new items hit the store shelves, arriving in tractor-trailer packed with suitcases from major airports.

I Guess You Had to Be There ...

In the middle of August in 1969, a stage was set up in a cow field in Bethel, New York. Advertised as "four days of peace, love, and music," by the time it was over, an estimated 400,000 people had descended upon the tiny town, and the event would go down in counter-culture history.

I'm talking, of course, about Woodstock.

Only those who attended know the true story of what went down there. But here are some fascinating, little-known facts about the rock concert people still talk about over 50 years later:

Plan "B" Brainchild. The event's organizers' original intent wasn't to have a music festival, but to create a recording studio. The idea somehow morphed into an outdoor rock concert. The name "Woodstock" was borrowed from a small town nearby that was already known as a destination for artists and music lovers.

Tossed Out by Toilets. The event was supposed to be held at Howard Mills Industrial Park in Middleton, New York. But residents didn't want it, fearing unruly crowds. They put the kibosh on it, claiming issues with the portable toilets that were to be used at the concert.

Saved by a Farmer. When the original venue fell through just a month before the event, a farmer named Max Yasgur stepped up and offered his 600-acre dairy farm. His speech welcoming Woodstock attendees is said to have gotten a standing ovation.

Airlifted Acts. The road into Bethel quickly turned into a nine-mile-long traffic jam. It was so awful that the opening band, Sweetwater, had to be airlifted in by helicopter. The band became the second act, after Richie Havens. To keep the crowd entertained, Havens sang and improvised for three hours until Sweetwater finally made it there.

Not a Rowdy Bunch. Despite the worries of concerned citizens, amongst the Woodstock crowd there were virtually no reports of violence. Interestingly, the man in charge of security wore a Smokey-the-Bear outfit and called himself Wavy Gravy. He supposedly threatened misbehavers with "fizzy water and custard pies."

It must've worked. The local chief of police, Lou Yank, declared the concertgoers, "the most courteous, considerate, and well-behaved group of kids I have ever been in contact with in my 24 years of police work."

Not-So-Deadly Drugs. The use of psychedelic drugs at the event resulted in 25 "freak-outs" every hour the first night of the event. Emergency medical staff, along with members of a New Mexico-based commune known as the Hog Farm, sat with stricken users until the drugs wore off. By the festival's end, 800 drug-related incidents were reported, but only two people died of overdoses.

Mass-Feeding Miracle. Inundated with a crowd exponentially larger than anticipated, the Hog Farm commune, originally hired to help keep the peace, stepped up and started recruiting new members to help cook and serve food. A local Jewish Community Center also sprang into action, providing thousands of sandwiches.

Then Governor Nelson Rockefeller declared the area a state of emergency in order to facilitate delivery of needed goods. The US Army airlifted thousands of pounds of food, water, and medical supplies to feed and care for the crowd.

Minding the PA System. During the event, there were public service announcements between each act. With no cell phones, it was the only way to get messages through to the crowd. The guy manning the microphone was named Edward "Chip" Monck.

Skipping Out on the Headliner. Due to, well, lots of reasons, the main headliner of the event, Jimi Hendrix, didn't appear on stage until 9 a.m. Monday morning. By the time he performed his historic rendition of *The Star-Spangled Banner*, over 90% of attendees had already left.

Fun Facts: Despite numerous rumors of births taking place during the festival, no evidence has surfaced to support any children being born at Woodstock. However, the event was definitely a financial bust. Woodstock cost an estimated $3 million, but only generated $1.8 million—due largely to the inability to collect admission fees. It took the concert's organizers until the early 1980s to pay off the debt.

Living Large in a Small Town

Lots of folks in small towns dream of life in the fast lane, in places like New York City, Los Angeles, or Miami. But for the residents of tiny Casey, Illinois, there's no need to move to the big city to live large. All they have to do is look out their windows.

You see, Casey, Illinois is home to a dozen of the world's largest ... *things*.

It all began after the completion of I-70 diverted a lot of traffic away from Casey and small towns like it. Seeking a way to lure folks back in and revitalize the town with tourism, they came up with what they call their "Big Things" project. In other words, their big idea was to build things big enough to beat world records.

Headed by Jim Bolin, construction on the first big thing began in late 2011. That's when the town of Casey set out to break the record for the ***world's largest wind chime***. They finished it, and clanged their way into a place in the history books. The 54-foot tall wind chime now stands along Main Street.

Another big idea, to build ***the world's largest golf tee,*** came from the local country club president. Work began on the wooden structure in July 2012, and took nearly a year to complete. At 30 feet tall and weighing in at 6.659 pounds, Casey had gained yet another "world's largest" thing.

In 2013, the town took on its biggest challenge by trying to break the record for the ***world's largest rocking chair***. The monster project took two years to build. To qualify for the record, the 42-foot tall chair actually had to rock. It took ten men to get all 46,200 pounds of it going, but the chair rocked, and another record was made in 2015.

In October of 2015, the town again gained status as home to the ***world's largest pair of wooden shoes***. Each one weighs in at 2,500 pounds, is 11 feet, five inches long, and can accommodate 15 people standing inside it! You'll find the humongous clogs inside a historic building downtown.

In 2014, a project to build the *world's largest pitchfork* got underway, having no previous contender to beat. To apply for a world record, an object has to be at least 10 times larger than normal. The town accomplished this and more with its 60-foot-long pitchfork. It weighs in at 1940 pounds and is stationed in front of Richard's Farm Restaurant.

To claim the title for *world's largest mailbox*, the box had to be fully operational. The gigantic one along Casey's Main Street is that and *then* some. With an interior of 5,743 cubic feet, visitors can climb stairs and post their own letters inside it! And, of course, a giant red flag goes up when there are letters to be picked up.

When the town set out to make the *world's largest key*, they decided to make it a modern version that looks like the straight metal post and plastic fob that come with today's cars. Standing at 28 feet, 2 inches, Casey's key is about the size of a gas station sign!

Continuing on their theme, the community also created the *world's largest gavel.* Placed in front of the courthouse in Marshall, it was the first joint project with the nearby town. The impressive gavel puts the hammer down at six feet, eight inches long and five feet high.

While you're in Casey, be sure and go by Brownie's Place to catch a glimpse of the *world's largest swizzle spoon*. It's 11 feet, 8.5 inches long. And stop by the barber shop to see the giant, 14 foot striped *spinning barbershop pole*.

Ever since the giant golf tee went up, townfolk kept asking about a super-sized golf club to go with it. Their wish was granted with the addition of the *world's largest golf driver*. Created with an old aluminum light pole and head of persimmon wood, it measures 45 feet long and weighs 731 pounds.

One of the most fun attractions in Casey is the *world's largest teeter-totter*. The giant seesaw is 82 feet long, and actually works! Visitors can ride the gentle giant every Saturday during tourist season.

Fun Fact: Besides having 12 of the world's largest things in the world, Casey also has over 20 other overgrown attractions for you to gawk your way through town at. They include: a pair of giant antlers, an anvil, a bat, a birdcage, a bookworm, a cactus, a crochet hook, an ear of corn, a glider plane, a horseshoe, knitting needles, a mouse trap, a nail puzzle, a pencil, a piggybank, a pizza slicer, a rocking horse, a spinning top, a wooden token, a yardstick, and my personal favorite—a huge taco.

The Toys of Christmas Past

Nowadays, it seems every child wants a new iPhone or Play Station in their holiday stocking. But before electronics took over, kids wrote Santa asking for quite a different set of toys.

Even so, just like today, nearly every kid wanted the same hot new toy that was all the rage that given year. These annual "toy crazes" led to a bunch of "crazed parents" scrambling to fulfill their darlings' Christmas wishes before supplies ran out.

Whether you were the parent or the kid, you might recall some of these holiday delights—and the shopping nightmares they generated. Ho ho ho!

Mr. Potato Head. Created as part of a cereal box promotion by George Lerner, the set of silly face parts were intended for kids to stick into real potatoes. Seeing its further potential, however, Hasbro acquired Lerner's creation.

In 1952 the company packaged together 28 parts, along with a Styrofoam head, and Mr. Potato Head was born. The toy tuber made history as the first children's toy advertised on TV. It sold more than a million units its first year. A year later, Mrs. Potato Head joined him in mushy matrimony.

Cabbage Patch Kids. Remember these soft-sculptured dolls? They were simple, made of cloth and vinyl, and if you ask me, kind of ugly with those puffy, potato-like faces of theirs. Still, the craze they created in 1983 was akin to some kind of voodoo spell. *Time* magazine reported near-riots breaking out among people vying to get their hands on one.

A 1,000-person crowd turned into a violent mob at one Pennsylvania department store. A woman suffered a broken leg and one store manager claimed "he armed himself with a baseball bat to defend his position behind the counter."

Tickle Me Elmo. This fuzzy red character from *Sesame Street* created a less-than-cute crisis for any parent trying to secure one for their child. Rosie O'Donnell featured the cuddly Muppet on her show in October 1996, creating a tsunami of public desire. Shopping frenzies ensued, including stampedes, scalpers, arrests, and injuries.

A Wal-Mart employee named Robert Waller told *People* magazine about the time his store received a late-night shipment of the coveted toy. He was caught in a human stampede. "I was pulled under, trampled—the crotch was yanked out of my brand-new blue jeans." Certainly no laughing matter, no matter how much you tickle Elmo.

Beanie Babies. When you think of "toy craze," this is usually the one that instantly comes to mind Their popularity in the 1990s couldn't be underestimated. Many people—both kids and adults—were convinced the bean-bag figures were a good investment. But the conceived "rarity" of many Beany Baby designs were a strategic marketing tactic by their manufacturer, Ty, Inc., who purposely limited quantities each store could keep in stock.

Furbys. If you were around in 1998, you couldn't escape the frenzy over Furbys. This part owl, part hamster, part mythical forest creature was *the* toy kids had to have or they might die. Why? Not only were Furbys cute, they spoke "Furbish," until they were "taught" English as their owners played with them.

Furbys were in such hot demand that holiday season that the original retail price nearly tripled—from $35 to $100. Despite the price hike, Tiger Electronics sold 1.8 million the first year, and an astounding 40 million during the original three years of their production.

Frozen Elsa Dolls. One of the latest "toy crazes" occurred in 2014. Following on the heels of the wildly successful movie, *Frozen*, this doll created shortages nationwide. At one point, the dolls were selling for up to $1000 apiece on eBay.

Disney stores had to place a two-item-per-customer "freeze" on the purchase of Elsa dolls. An employee at Disney's Times Square location told the *New York Post* that "physical fights" broke out over the dolls. Thankfully, the manufacturer addressed the shortage crisis. Shelves were restocked by the holidays, helping many a parent avoid the "cold shoulder" by disappointed kiddos.

Fun Fact: The board game Monopoly was patented by Charles Darrow. When it hit the shelves in 1936, it was a smash hit. It still is. According to Guinness records, Monopoly is still the most played board game in the world.

Jellyfish Fields Forever

Want to live forever? Be careful what you ask for. You could be reincarnated as a spineless, gelatinous blob. No, I don't mean like my creepy Uncle Gary. I mean like a jellyfish—specifically, a *Turritopsis dohrnii*.

Huh? Scientists in Spain studying this jellyfish have unlocked its genetic code—one that allows it to repeatedly revert into a juvenile state. (Kind of like my ex.) Anyway, why is that important? Because this particular trait could unlock the secret to *T. dohrnii's* unique longevity, which could then help us discover clues to help humans live longer, too.

Like other types of jellyfish, *T. dohrnii* goes through a two-part life cycle. First, it survives in an asexual phase, where its chief goal is to find enough to eat. Then, when conditions are right, it reproduces sexually. (Insert your own joke here.)

Looking like tiny, translucent umbrellas, *T. dohrnii* are the size of lentils. What makes them so special is that if their bodies are damaged, the mature adults (called medusas) can transform back into their youthful selves! To do so, they first shed their limbs and become drifting blobs that morph back into larval polyps. Gradually, the once-injured medusa buds off the polyp as a fully formed and rejuvenated adult.

Though many types of jellyfish have some capacity to reverse aging and revert to a larval stage, most lose that ability after they reach sexual maturity. But *T. dohrnii* can do this seemingly forever, earning it the nickname of the immortal jellyfish.

While a medusa can be killed by being either eaten or too severely injured, it will never die of old age. It will simply rejuvenate itself in perpetuity, making it, in a way, immortal.

How is this possible? What scientists have discovered is that *T. dohrnii* has variations in its genome that make it better at copying and repairing DNA. The species also appears to be better at maintaining and repairing the ends of chromosomes, called telomeres. (These ends can be damaged and shortened during cell reproduction, leading to aging and mutation.)

While this probably won't lead to a jellyfish fountain of youth, it might help us learn how protein functionality works, and how it helps the jellyfish cheat death.

Fun Fact: One of the most important scientific findings of the last century was the discovery of an immortal human cell line. It was identified by Johns Hopkins researcher Dr. George Gey in 1951. Known as "HeLa cells," they were named after the cancer patient they came from, Henrietta Lacks. Hardy and quick reproducing, this same remarkably resilient and prolific cell line continues to be used in labs today, and has become a workhorse for biological research.

Want a Pack of Product Placements to Go with that Popcorn?

You might think that actors plugging products in movies is a new thing. But the first one actually occurred way back in 1920. *The Garage*, starring Roscoe "Fatty" Arbuckle, took place mainly in a service station selling Red Crown Gasoline.

This film cemented the connection between star appeal and product sales. The practice took off. Today, there are three kinds of product placements:

- Screen placement—where the brand is seen in a shot, like Elliott laying down Reese's Pieces for the alien in *E.T.*
- Script placement—when a character says the product name, like Marty McFly ordering a Pepsi in *Back to the Future*.
- Plot placement—when the product or brand has some relation to the film's plot, such as Taco Bell being named as the only restaurant chain remaining in the future in *Demolition Man*, or the Aston Martin DB5 driven by James Bond in pretty much all the Bond films.

Getting all three types of placements in one scene is the holy trinity for any brand. It rarely happens, but even striking one or two can still be quite effective, as evidenced by the dollars advertisers are willing to pay to have a movie character flaunt their brands. Check out these examples:

- M&Ms were supposed to be featured in *E.T.*, but they pulled out. Hershey's stepped in, paying a cool million dollars to showcase Reese's Pieces. E.T. was a hit—and so was the candy. Sales increase a whopping 65% the year after the film's release.
- In the 2012 Bond film *Skyfall*, James Bond takes a sip of beer. Heineken picked up the bar tab—paying $45 million for the product plug.
- In 1992, Jack Daniel's paid over a million dollars to have the main characters in *Basic Instinct* drink their whiskey (and no one else's). The scene between Michael Douglas and Sharon Stone lasted just a

few seconds, but resulted in a five-fold increase in sales of Jack
Daniel's products.

- When *The Matrix* released in 1999, Nokia sold more than 8 million of the 8110 phone used by hacker Neo, played by Keanu Reeves.
- Seven months after the premiere of *Top Gun* in 1986, sales of Ray-Ban sunglasses like the ones worn by Maverick (played by Tom Cruise) were up 40%.

Product placement isn't just a way for greedy producers to get more money for their films. With the high cost of production, advertisers are becoming an important way to shore up a film's budget. So, it's probably a safe bet to say it's not going away anytime soon.

Fun Fact: Sometimes product placement just happens, as in the movie *My Big Fat Greek Wedding*. The father of the film's writer and star, Nia Vardalos, swore that Windex helped get rid of a wart on his hand. Amused, she wrote the quirk into the script.

The character that plays her father in the film claims that Windex can cure poison ivy, psoriasis, and baldness—as well as warts. The Windex manufacturers didn't mind the free placement one bit. They claimed product sales were noticeably up after the film released.

No More Funny Business!

You're reading this book, so I already know you like to laugh. But what about the people who attempt to eke out a living trying to make us laugh? Below are an assortment of surprising and weird facts about some of America's favorite comedians:

Jerry Seinfeld was actually banned from the restaurant that inspired "The Soup Nazi," an iconic *Seinfeld* episode. The restaurateur hated the way his strict ordering rules were portrayed on the show.

In 2001, *Robin Williams* appeared on an episode of *Inside the Actors Studio*. Apparently, during the set he made one audience member laugh so hard they actually got a hernia and had to be taken away in an ambulance at the end of the show.

Comedian *Wanda Sykes* used to work for the National Security Agency (NSA). As a contracting specialist, she had top-secret security clearance.

In 2004, *Dave Chappelle* spoofed Prince in a skit on *Chappelle's Show*. Prince liked it so much he used the photo of Chappelle dressed up as him on the album cover of his single, *Breakfast Can Wait*.

Mindy Kaling's full name is Vera Mindy Chokalingam. Her parents named her partly after the show *Mork & Mindy*, a sitcom they watched on TV.

Stephen Colbert had a Ben & Jerry's flavor named for him—"Americone Dream." He donates all the money he makes from sales to fund "food and medical assistance for disadvantaged children, helping veterans and their families, and environmental causes."

In 2007, *Steve Martin* married Anne Stringfield in a surprise ceremony. The 75 guests, many celebrities, were told it was just a normal party. Lorne Michaels, the creator of *Saturday Night Live*, was the best man.

Before *Trevor Noah* took the job, *Amy Schumer* was asked to take over hosting *The Daily Show*. She said she was honored to be asked, but ultimately turned it down. Her reason? She likes not knowing what she's going to do next.

Comedian *Jon Stewart* worked out a unique way to propose to his girlfriend. He had Will Shortz, the crossword puzzle editor for the *New York Times*, create a personalized crossword to help him pop the question.

In 2015, *Jim Gaffigan* was asked to perform stand-up comedy for Pope Francis at the Festival of Families in Philadelphia. Gaffigan joked that the whole while he kept waiting for an organizer to apologize and explain they'd gotten him mixed up with Stephen Colbert.

Fun Fact: When *Richard Pryor* hosted *Saturday Night Live* in 1975, NBC executives were worried he was "too dangerous" for live TV. They instigated a 5-second delay to stop any bad language before it aired. The tactic soon became standard practice, and is still used for most live TV today.

Hats Off to Pioneering Moms

Not everyone was born under a lucky star. In fact, some folks' rise to fame and fortune are downright dumbfounding and miraculous. Take a look at the amazing story of one woman who carved a whole new path for women in the US. Can you guess who she is?

Loretta Mary Aiken was a fated woman from the day she was born, which was March 19, 1894—or thereabouts, as no one is quite sure anymore. Of modest means, her father, a firefighter, died in an explosion when she was just 11. Not long afterward, her mother was hit and killed by a truck on Christmas Day. In her teens, poor Loretta was raped twice and became pregnant both times, having to give her children away because of social and financial circumstances.

Given her horrific childhood, you would think Loretta would have given up on life, and turned into a bitter, cheerless victim. But she had other ideas. Instead of wallowing in self-pity, at the age of 14 (and with encouragement from her grandmother) Loretta up and joined the circus—I mean the *circuit*.

The African American vaudeville circuit, to be exact. And what was her talent? Incredibly, it was *comedy*.

Loretta borrowed her stage name from a fellow performer, Jack Mabley, and became Jackie Mabley. Her reputation on the circuit as a mothering spirit eventually led to her being called "Moms." But it was Loretta's raw, comedic talent that led her to become Moms Mabley, the trailblazing African American comedian famous for her warm, yet raunchy stand-up routines.

At her shows, Mabley presented herself as a dowdy, older lady in a simple housedress and floppy hat. Her penchant for handsome young men rather than "old, washed-up geezers," became a signature bit for her. Offstage, however, Mabley was quite the opposite. In person she kept a glamorous, chic look, and her sexual preference was toward women. (She was one of the first openly gay comedians.)

Mabley's comic genius made her a regular attraction at the Cotton Club. In 1931, she entered the world of film and stage. She worked with writer Zora Neale Hurston on the Broadway show, *Fast and Furious: A Colored Revue in 37 Scenes*. In 1933, she took on a feature role in Paul Robeson's film, *The Emperor Jones*.

But that was just the beginning of Moms Mabley's rise to stardom. In the late 1930s, she became the first woman comedian to be featured at the Apollo theater in Harlem. After that, Mabley appeared at the Apollo more times than any other performer—a testament to her talent and popularity.

Mabley went on to star in numerous films, including the 1948 movie, *Killer Diller*, which featured Nat King Cole and Butterfly McQueen. In the 1960s, she was producing hit comedy albums with Chess Records. Her debut album, *The Funniest Woman Alive*, became gold-certified.

During that time, Mabley had also become a top draw for numerous TV variety shows, including:

- *The Smothers Brothers Comedy Hour* (1967)
- *The Ed Sullivan Show* (1969)
- *The Merv Griffin Show* (1969)
- *The Bill Cosby Show* (1970)
- *The Pearl Bailey Show* (1971)

Quite an amazing list of accomplishments for a woman with such a hard beginning, don't you think? Instead of practicing sadness, Moms Maabley practiced happiness. Her efforts even got her to Carnegie Hall in 1962. Well done, Moms. Well done.

Fun Fact: While Moms Mabley passed away in 1975, she lives on in film and stage—literally. Actress Clarice Taylor (who played the mother on *The Cosby Show*) portrayed the iconic comedian in the 1987 play, *Moms*, at the Astor Place Theater. In 2019, Moms also appeared in the final episode of the third season of the TV series, *The Marvelous Mrs. Maisel*, set in the late 1950s. Moms portrayed by comedian Wanda Sykes, who performs a full stand-up routine at the Apollo.

Random Acts of Weirdness

Since this book is designed to help celebrate the weird and wonderful, I've included a veritable grab-bag of weird facts that are fascinating, but didn't related to any of the other stories in the book. Enjoy!

◇ The Great Wall of China was held together with lime, water, and sticky rice.

◇ PEZ candy was invented to help people quit smoking cigarettes. The original dispensers were shaped similar to a cigarette lighter.

◇ Humans take an average of 22,000 breaths a day.

◇ Bananas glow blue under UV lights.

◇ The word SWIMS is still SWIMS when turned upside down.

◇ Cheese is the most shoplifted food in the world.

◇ In the US, there are more vacant houses than homeless people.

◇ Dining at one place each day, it would take 22.7 years to eat at every restaurant in New York City.

◇ Dogs typically poop in alignment with the north-south axis.

◇ During the Stone Age, the entire population of Central Europe could have fit on a small cruise ship. (Only around 1,500 people!)

◇ Humans are born with just one pint of blood, but by the time we're adults we have four to five quarts.

◇ Lobsters used to be so cheap that they were used to feed prisoners.

◇ The human body contains enough fat to make seven bars of soap. (Life Boy, perhaps?)

◈ When it came out in the 1960s, Twister was considered a risqué game.

◈ Your feet can sweat up to 20 liters per year.

◈ Your thumb doesn't make a sound when you snap your fingers. What you hear is your middle finger hitting your palm.

◈ It's impossible to hum while holding your nose. (Go ahead. Try!)

◈ Beer was legally classified as a soft drink in Russia until 2011.

◈ A dog's sense of smell is so good that it can detect a teaspoon of sugar in a million gallons of water.

◈ Platypuses are weird enough with their bird-like bill and webbed feet, but another little-known fact is they don't have stomachs! Their gullets connect directly to their intestines.

◈ Tomatoes are native to the Americas. That means there was no such thing as tomato sauce in Italy until at least the 16th century.

◈ Human stomach acid is strong enough to dissolve metal.

◈ The wasabi paste you get in a sushi restaurant probably isn't wasabi at all, but horseradish.

◈ Human babies are born without "kneecaps," as we know them. Instead, they have cartilaginous structures in their knees which turn to bone by the age of four.

Fun Fact: During WWII, a US plane carrying nine men crashed on the Japanese island of Chi Chi Jima. Eight of the men were captured and eaten by cannibals. The only one who escaped and was later rescued went on to become the 41st President of the United States, George H.W. Bush.

Big Stars, Small Paychecks

Before they started hauling in the big bucks, would-be stars had to pay their dues—some more than others, as you're about to find out:

Dustin Hoffman reportedly was paid just $17,000 for his breakout role in *The Graduate* in 1968. The role earned him an Academy Award nomination for best actor.

Actor and comedian *John Candy* had starring roles in *Splash*, *Spaceballs*, and *Uncle Buck*. But before that, he was offered a cameo role in *Home Alone*, for which he was paid a measly $414.

Actress *Hilary Swank* was paid just $3,000 for her Oscar-winning role in *Boys Don't Cry*. (But maybe girls do.)

Jamie Lee Curtis was paid $2,000 a week while filming her role in the movie *Halloween*. She netted $8,000 for the project, and bought her character's costume at JC Penney.

For his Oscar-nominated role in *Half Nelson*, *Ryan Gosling* earned just $1,000 a week.

Bill Murray earned a paltry $9,000 for his work on *Rushmore* in 1998.

For his work in *Thelma and Louise*, a young *Brad Pitt* was paid just $6,000. Think that's bad? In 2018, for his role in *Deadpool 2*, Pitt agreed to work for scale—and a cup of coffee. For his cameo role he earned a Starbucks and a whopping $956.

Oprah Winfrey was paid just $35,000 for her starring role in *The Color Purple*. The whole while, she was terrified she'd be fired from the film "because I didn't know what I was doing. Period," she told the *LA Times* in 2017. Winfrey shouldn't have worried. The movie earned her a best-supporting actress nod at the 1986 Academy Awards.

Taking an offer he actually wanted to refuse, *Al Pacino* earned just $35,000 for his iconic role in *The Godfather*.

In 1979, *Mel Gibson* earned an unimpressive $15,000 for the lead role in *Mad Max*.

Harrison Ford wasn't exactly over the moon with his $10,000 payday playing Hans Solo in *Star Wars*.

Fun Fact: Miniscule paychecks aren't just a thing of the past. New actors and actresses still take small pay in hopes of becoming big stars. For instance, actor Jon Heder was paid a mere $1,000 for his starring role in the 2004 film, *Napoleon Dynamite*.

The movie went on to gross over $40 million in the US alone. But don't feel bad for Heder. As the movie's success grew, so did his paycheck. "They went a little bit higher," Heder hinted, when asked about renegotiating the contract.

Things You Really Don't Want to Know

I'm kind of serious about that headline. Don't read any further if you're squeamish. Don't say I didn't warn you!

Here goes...last chance to turn the page before it's too late:

- In ten years, the average mattress will weigh double what it did, due to accumulation of dust mites and their excrement.
- Most laugh tracks used for TV sitcoms were recorded in the 1950s, so you're probably listening to dead people laughing.
- A single sneeze travels 100 miles per hour and shoots 100,000 germs into the air.
- Dentures were once routinely made out of actual human or animal teeth.
- Ancient Romans brushed their teeth with mouse brains and used urine to whiten them.
- A major source of red food coloring is crushed cochineal beetles.
- Bloody Mary cocktails may have gotten their name from Queen Mary of England. She had hundreds of people burned at the stake.
- Human lips are made of the same skin type and texture as our anuses.
- The average person unintentionally consumes a pound of insects a year, usually mixed into other foods.
- The apples you buy in the grocery store could be over a year old.
- Depending on which brand of toilet paper you use, fecal matter can get through up to ten layers.
- Over 40,000 parasites and 250 kinds of bacteria can be exchanged in a single kiss.
- FDA regulations allow 10 insects and 35 fruit-fly eggs per eight ounces of raisins, and 150 bug fragments and five rodent hairs per pound of peanut butter.
- Over 200 frozen corpses lie along hiking trails on Mount Everest. Climbers use them as "way points" to determine their locations.
- Fully 15% of the air you breathe in an average metro station is comprised of human skin.

- There have been multiple cases of people actually being "eaten" by escalators.
- Your cellphone, kitchen sink, desk, grocery cart, and restaurant menu all have more bacteria on them than your toilet bowl.

Fun Fact: Thank goodness, this list is over. And believe it or not, I spared you from some even *more* gruesome facts. You're welcome.

The Dude Really Does Abide

It may be hard to believe, but there's a religion that was inspired by ... *a movie*. I don't mean a cultish offshoot from some bizarre horror movie. I'm talking about a philosophy of life inspired by Jeffrey "The Dude" Lebowski, the main protagonist in the 1998 film, *The Big Lebowski*.

Played by Jeff Bridges, The Dude's laid-back, pacifist attitude and penchant for wearing a bathrobe just about anywhere somehow gave rise to the Church of the Latter-Day Dudes, and the belief in Dudeism.

Founded in 2005 by Oliver Benjamin, a journalist based in Chiang Mai, Thailand, Dudeism advocates and encourages the practice of "going with the flow," "being cool-headed," and "taking it easy" when facing life's difficulties. Followers believe this is the only way to live in harmony with our inner nature and the challenges wrought by interacting with other people.

Another important aspect of Dudesim is to assuage feelings of inadequacy that arise in societies that place a heavy emphasis on achievement and personal fortune. Instead, conscripts are encouraged to enjoy simple, everyday pleasures such as bowling, bathing, and hanging out with friends. They see it as far preferable to striving to accumulate wealth and buying things as a means to achieve happiness and fulfillment.

A famous line from the move, "the dude abides," encourages followers to relax, enjoy simple pleasures, and be generally tolerant of others. It also advocates maintaining calm in the face of adversity, and encouraging others to do the same.

Though seen by some as a "mock religion," Dudeism's laid-back philosophies have struck a harmonious chord with quite a lot of people. As of May 2017, the "church" had ordained over 450,000 Dudeist priests around the world!

Interested in becoming a Dudeist? They offer a free, online university where interested dudes can obtain honorary degrees. Or you might want to check out *The Abide Guide*. Written by Benjamin and the Arch Dudeship Dwayne Eutsey, the Dudeist self-help book was published in August 2011, and provides tips on living like Lebowski.

All I can say is, may "The Dude" be with you.

Fun Fact: March 6 is the annual sacred holy day for Dudeism. It marks, of course, The Day of the Dude.

A Special Thank You

Dear Reader,

Thank you so much for reading the second installment of Interesting Stories for Curious Minds. I hope you learned a lot, and laughed even more!

Want to keep the fun going? You can!

Simply join my Facebook group and you'll receive a giggle a day in your Facebook feed!

To join, go to Facebook and search for Margaret Lashley – Author. Or simply click the link below and sign up.

https://www.facebook.com/valandpalspage

Either way, I hope to see you there soon!

All my best,

Margaret

More Books by Margaret Lashley

Available at margaretlashley.com or on Amazon in Your Choice of Ebook, Paperback, Hardback, or Audiobook:

- Doreen Diller Mystery Trilogy (Three-Book Series)
- Val Fremden Midlife Mysteries (Nine-Book Series)
- Absolute Zero (The Val Fremden Prequel)
- Freaky Florida Investigations (Eight-Book Series)
- Mind's Eye Investigators (Two-Book Series)

www.ingramcontent.com/pod-product-compliance
Lightning Source LLC
Chambersburg PA
CBHW072021040426
42447CB00009B/1682